Beside the Sea

A Play

Brian Jefferies

Samuel French — London
New York — Sydney — Toronto — Hollywood

BESIDE THE SEA

Beside the Sea was first produced by the Bristol Old Vic Company at the Theatre Royal, Bristol on 11th March 1981, with the following cast of characters:

Jack Mercer	Bill Wallis
Beryl, his wife	Barbara Young
Freda, his daughter	Julia Hills
Malcolm, his son	Kenneth Price
Maurice Adamson	Peter Copley
Helen, his wife	June Barrie
Sarah, his daughter	Linsey Beauchamp
Arnold	Ian Mackenzie

Directed by Anthony Cornish
Designed by Belinda Ackermann

The action takes place on a beach during one day in summer

SCENE 1   8.30 a.m.
SCENE 2   11.30 a.m.
SCENE 3   2.30 p.m.
SCENE 4   4.30 p.m.

Time—the present

SCENE 1

The scene is an impression of a sandy beach. 8.30 a.m.

A long and wide stretch of sand slopes from rear to front stage. Beyond the beach—a blue sky. There is the sound of the sea

Arnold enters. He is a man in his early thirties; lean and sunburned. His clothes are tidy but overworn and slightly eccentric. On his head is a sagging broad-brimmed straw hat. He carries a hessian carrier-bag. Arnold is searching the beach for items of interest. He kneels down and picks up a piece of split tree branch that has been bleached, smoothed and discarded several times by the sea. He examines it closely; running his fingers around the shape with a certain sensitivity

Arnold The unfolding tide leaves her story on the sand. (*He pauses*) O shape of wood, what is your story? (*His delivery is always theatrical, varying by degrees to suit the mood*)

Maurice enters from the rear of the beach. He is a man in his middle to late fifties, neatly dressed in expensive but outdated casual-wear

Standing at the rear of the beach, Maurice looks first at Arnold and then at the seascape. Arnold has not seen him. Maurice begins to move slowly down the beach

(*Sensing Maurice's presence*) Good-morning.
Maurice Oh . . . Good-morning.
Arnold (*turning his head slowly*) It's a lovely day. (*He re-examines the piece of wood*)
Maurice Yes. Yes, it is. (*After a short pause*) I've been watching you from that cliff up there.

No reaction from Arnold

I could see you quite clearly. (*He shades his eyes and peers into the high distance*) Amazing really. (*He hesitates*) Being the only one on the beach made you all the more obvious.
Arnold (*distantly*) Yes, I see. I see what you mean.

Silence, apart from the sound of the sea. Arnold continues to examine the wood from various angles. Maurice surveys the distance

O shape of wood, what is your story?
Maurice I beg your pardon?
Arnold (*considering the wood*) This is an interesting piece of wood. (*He pauses*) You're here on holiday?
Maurice Yes, I am. (*He pauses*) I left my family having their breakfast— at the hotel.

Arnold Ah. Where do you reside when you're not on holiday?

Maurice Where do I . . .? Oh, I see what you mean. Surrey. I live in Surrey.

Arnold Surrey! Is that a posh way of saying London?

Maurice No. No, it's not. As a matter of fact, I live at Oxted.

Arnold Oxted! (*Thoughtfully*) Frederick Delius is buried near there.

Maurice Is he? I didn't know that.

Arnold There are not many people who do. (*He pauses*) The sea is very calm.

Maurice It's a very pleasant morning. Very pleasant indeed.

Arnold There is something different about the morning. Have you noticed that? All the sounds are distinctive and clear. If I was suddenly placed upon this planet, I would know that it was morning—just by the quality of the sounds. (*He looks at Maurice*) Have you ever been aware of the morning sounds?

Maurice No, I don't think so.

Arnold Then I would advise you to listen more carefully. (*He pauses*) You must think me very odd?

Maurice (*considering*) In a way, yes.

Arnold Right! Old straw hat, tatty clothes—combing the beach. You must think I'm a tramp.

Maurice Well, I wouldn't say . . .

Arnold Why not? I look like a tramp. But I am not a tramp—have no fear. I am merely on the beach searching for interesting shapes—like this piece of wood. I'm fascinated with the shapes the sea can mould.

Maurice That's very interesting.

Arnold You think so?

Maurice Yes. Yes, I do.

Arnold Good. Sit down and listen to the morning sounds. The beach is free, and is free of people—for a short time. Soon they'll be here—the holidaymakers. Most of them never look at the beauty of a beach. They just dig at it—scuff it—kick it—litter it and let their children pee on it. Come on! Come on! Sit down.

Maurice (*slightly overwhelmed*) I will. Thank you. Just for a short while. (*He squats next to Arnold*)

For a few moments they stare at the sea

Arnold D'you know, there's something very interesting about holiday attire.

Maurice becomes conscious of his clothes

In revealing the body they hide the man. They are an unconscious disguise—or a conscious disguise—or subconscious—or even a self-conscious disguise.

Maurice (*not impressed but amused*) You think so?

Arnold I know so. Holiday clothes—a great leveller of social status. But the experienced eye can see through all that. You cannot completely hide breeding. Take yourself . . . I would say . . . looking at you . . . I

would say—and I could be wrong—but I doubt it . . . you are a chief
clerk in a bank—or at the best, an assistant manager.

Maurice I am an accountant.

Arnold Chartered?

Maurice Yes.

Arnold In a bank?

Maurice No.

Arnold Then I was all but right. I'm rarely wrong——

Maurice You were very close.

Arnold—because I am constantly studying human nature—and the human
state. It is an essential part of my work.

Maurice Really? (*He pauses*) What exactly are you?

Arnold What am I? Is it not obvious? I, my friend, am a poet!

Maurice A poet! Really?

No reply from Arnold

You're a poet? That's your job?

Arnold I'm not sure that I care for the word—job.

Maurice (*amused*) Oh, I see. I'm sorry. A poet! My wife would be very
interested—and may even be impressed if she were here. She's very keen
on that sort of thing.

Arnold What sort of thing?

Maurice Poetry . . . that sort of thing.

Arnold Oh.

Maurice Music, theatre, Gilbert and Sullivan . . .

Arnold Gilbert and Sullivan!

Maurice Yes. She's very keen on Gilbert and Sullivan.

Arnold Ah, good. I would like to meet your wife—she sounds a special
lady. (*He pauses*) Can you tell me the time?

Maurice Yes. It's two minutes to nine o'clock.

Arnold Then I must be going. (*He stands*) There are things to be done.
It's been a pleasant experience meeting you—Mr——?

Maurice Adamson. Maurice Adamson (*He stands up*)

Arnold Pleasure meeting you, Maurice. See you again perhaps.

Maurice Yes, I hope so. (*He offers his hand*)

They shake hands

Oh, by the way.

Arnold Yes?

Maurice What is your name?

Arnold Arnold.

Maurice Arnold. Is that your first name?

Arnold First name, second name and third. Goodbye. (*He begins to move
away*)

Maurice Oh, by the way . . .

Arnold Yes?

Maurice That—that piece of wood. Is there something special about it?

Arnold Very. Very special indeed. It's the Taj Mahal, Madonna and

Child, Genesis, Alpha and Omega—time itself. You can have it. See for yourself. (*He hands him the piece of wood*) Goodbye again.

Arnold moves off and exits

Maurice's gaze alternates between the piece of wood and the departing Arnold

Jack Mercer enters. He is in his late forties, well-built, suntanned and wearing fashionable leisure-wear including shorts and a sun-hat. He is skilfully laden with multicoloured equipment for the beach, including sun-loungers, wind-shields, a folding table, deflated inflatables and a kit-bag full of bats, balls, racquets, shuttlecocks, etc.

Jack (*to Maurice; heartily*) Good-morning!
Maurice Good-morning.
Jack It's a grand morning.
Maurice Yes—yes it is. (*He is still glancing at Arnold's point of exit*)

Jack methodically unloads his burden; laying each item precisely on the beach. In Jack's handling of the equipment there is evidence of a well-tried and practised plan. Maurice becomes increasingly interested

Jack You're on the beach early?
Maurice Yes, I am. (*Giving more attention to Jack*) Actually, I'm just out for a walk.
Jack I see you were talking to Arnold.
Maurice Yes. You know him?
Jack Everybody knows Arnold.
Maurice Then he's famous.
Jack Famous? (*Amused*) In a way, I suppose he is.
Maurice I just told him that my wife will be upset . . .
Jack Oh?
Maurice Not meeting him.
Jack You've not seen Arnold before then?
Maurice No. We've just arrived. Last night.
Jack Your first time here for a holiday?
Maurice Yes, this is the first time.

Jack is continuing the arrangement of beach equipment

Jack Then why will she be upset?
Maurice Umm?
Jack Your wife.
Maurice Oh! Well, you see, she is extremely interested in poetry—all the arts of course, but poetry in particular.
Jack What has that to do with Arnold?
Maurice He being a poet.
Jack A poet? Arnold? He's not a poet! I'm sorry, but he's the chap who gives out the deck chairs.
Maurice Deck chairs?
Jack That's right. At the far end of the beach, that's where the deck

chairs are. He gives them out—takes the money and makes the refunds when you take them back. Everybody on the beach knows Arnold, of course they do.

Maurice He told me he was a poet.

Jack He's pulling the other one.

Maurice Pardon?

Jack He's pulling your leg.

Maurice (*thoughtfully*) Oh, I don't know about that. (*He peers in the direction of Arnold's exit*)

Jack continues the process of setting up by driving in the stakes of the windshields. Maurice examines the piece of wood

Jack I could tell that you were a new arrival—by the way you're bleached.

Maurice looks at him

You're looking pale. See what I mean?

Maurice (*thoughtfully*) Are you sure he's—he's what you say he is?

Jack Arnold? Of course I'm sure. I'm telling you. (*He sees the piece of driftwood*) Are you collecting wood?

Maurice (*still deep in thought*) No . . . no, I'm not. (*He looks at the wood*) Tell me, what d'you see in this piece of wood?

Jack (*stopping work*) What d'you mean? That piece? (*He moves to Maurice*)

Maurice What do you see in it?

Jack That?

Maurice If anything?

Jack It's a piece of driftwood.

Maurice Anything more?

Jack No. (*He takes the wood from Maurice*) Driftwood—piece of a tree— not long out of the water—been in the water a long time, I would guess. Is it supposed to be something else?

Maurice (*amused*) The Taj Mahal?

Jack (*not understanding the question*) I can't see anything. It's a piece of wood. (*He returns the wood*) Can you?

Maurice No.

Jack (*returning to his task*) I must get on with the work in hand, or the wife'll be after me.

Maurice discards the piece of wood on to the beach

Throughout the action of the play the characters occasionally pick up the piece of driftwood and examine it—sometimes consciously and sometimes unconsciously—before discarding it to the sand

Maurice watches Jack at work with increasing interest

Maurice You're on the beach early.

Jack Always here early. Same spot on the beach every day. I'm always first—to claim the pitch. The rest of the family bring up the rear. Bit of a family beach routine—if you see what I mean.

Maurice You certainly have a lot of equipment.

Jack I like to do the job properly. Self-sufficient, I think that's the word for it. You have to be self-sufficient at this end of the beach, oh yes. This is the quiet end. No facilities. Deck chairs, café and toilets are all at that end. Not many people get up as far as this. Just a few— just a few. Enough to make it feel . . . well, you know, not lonely. Quieter and more room—if you see what I mean.

Maurice Yes. Yes, I do.

Jack Nice here, don't you think? Pleasant spot.

Maurice You've been here for some time, on holiday?

Jack This is our third week. Going home the day after tomorrow.

Maurice Ah, that is sad.

There is a short pause

Jack You're venturing on the beach then?

Maurice Oh yes, we like the beach. Not every day. When it's warm . . . not too hot. When it's warm.

Jack I love the beach. It's funny really—have you ever thought what it is about a beach? What makes people flock to it like sheep, when the sun comes out? And some of us are here when the sun stays in. Is it the sand? Kids like the sand. It gives your feet a free kind of feeling. Fields are not the same as sand—to the feet. (*He pauses*) Are you coming on the beach today?

Maurice Yes, I think so.

Jack Then I should come down to this spot. We can save you a pitch. Not that there's many people.

Maurice (*after a short consideration*) My wife prefers it quiet—and so do I. I think she would like it here.

Jack I'm sure she would. It would be a pleasure to have your company.

Maurice Yes. Yes, I think it would be nice. I will see what my wife and daughter think about it. (*He pauses*) I'll be going now . . . they'll be waiting for me.

Jack Where are you staying?

Maurice The *Metropole*.

Jack Ah, that's a nice place. Not too far away.

Maurice No . . . (*He lingers*)

Jack Right then! Off you go!

Maurice Yes . . . off I go! See you later on—maybe.

Jack Right! Hope so.

Maurice exits

Jack intently watches Maurice's withdrawal, smiles, then continues with the erection of his encampment. Wind-shield posts are knocked in, sun-loungers and chairs unfolded

> *Beryl enters dressed in fashionable sun-wear. She too is burdened and carries overfilled bags with rolled towels, etc. She is in her mid-forties*

Beryl Well, I'm here!

Jack Ah!

Beryl The family pack-horse.

Jack (*cheerfully*) I wouldn't say that. I didn't see you coming.

Beryl Couldn't you hear me puffing?

Jack Heard the noise, but couldn't place it.

Beryl I told your mother, before we came on holiday, her son married a pack-horse. (*She unloads*) You were too busy talking to that—who was that?

Jack Him! Didn't say his name. I didn't tell him mine, come to that. Odd sort really. He was carrying a piece of wood.

Beryl (*without interest*) What wood?

Jack Got it in his hand . . . He asked me some sort of question about it.

Beryl A question! He might be from one of those Sunday papers. You could have won a prize. Did you give him an answer?

Jack Not really—it was a silly question.

Beryl He may have been from the *News of the World*.

Jack I don't think so.

Beryl You don't know. D'you remember, last year, there was that girl from the *News of the World*—asking three simple questions?

Jack *The People*.

Beryl Um?

Jack She was from *The People*.

Beryl I thought it was the *News of the World*——

Jack *The People*.

Beryl —but it doesn't matter. Lots of people were winning prizes. (*She surveys the encampment*) You haven't done much here. (*She joins Jack in the task of assembling and arranging*)

Jack Where's Freda and Malcolm? Are they carrying anything?

Beryl They're coming. They're on their way. Malcom's fetching the newspapers.

Jack They can't be carrying much—it's nearly all here. It's the same every morning. It's us who do all the carrying, and our dear children just carry themselves.

Beryl But it's our fault. That's how we've brought them up.

Jack (*stopping*) Now that's a funny phrase when you come to think of it.

Beryl What is?

Jack Brought them up—when you think about it—like being sick.

Beryl Jack—that's vile!

Jack (*amused*) I'm sorry about that, but it's a funny phrase—you must agree.

Beryl I don't agree. Is the wind-shield facing the right way? It was windy yesterday.

Jack No wind at all today. It's going to be hot—and what breeze there is, is blowing this way. (*He licks his finger and raises it to sense the breeze*) Did those two kids of ours offer to carry anything?

Beryl Freda's carrying something—and Malcolm's getting the newspapers—I told you that.

Jack Marvellous isn't it! We bring them down here for a holiday . . .

Malcolm does nothing but read books all day, and Freda—Freda we hardly ever see. I pay for everything and there's little thanks.

Beryl But they came with us—which is something.

Jack And so they should. (*Looking into the distance*) There's no wind worth mentioning.

Beryl It's going to be hot.

Jack I said that just now.

Beryl Did you?

They continue with their routine of setting up. The loungers are in a row facing the sea. Beryl adds the towels to the layout

Jack That fellow I was talking to . . .

Beryl What one?

Jack The one who asked the questions. I told you . . .

Beryl Oh, yes. Are you sure he wasn't from the *News of the World*—or the *Daily Mirror* or something?

Jack I told him we would save them a place on the beach.

Beryl (*surprised*) Who? Did you? There's always plenty of room at this end. Why did you bother?

Jack He seemed a good sort—that's all. A bit on the posh side may be. He's got a wife and family.

Beryl Oh! You didn't tell me that.

Jack One daughter . . . I think . . . I think so.

Beryl Could be a friend for one of ours. That would be nice.

Jack Could be. They're staying at the *Metropole*.

Beryl Oh, I say—that is posh.

Jack We'll lay a few towels out over there to stake a claim. (*He picks up two towels*)

Beryl Jack, not those towels—they're a bit shabby. Put these new ones out. (*She replaces the towels*)

Jack Beryl, it's not that they're . . .

Beryl I'll put these down. (*She places the towels*) Have you actually invited them down?

Jack I just said it was the quiet end—and they like it quiet.

Beryl Well, I hope they're all right.

Jack He's all right. Decent sort.

Beryl If he goes about asking funny questions—I'm not so sure.

Malcolm and Freda enter. Freda, who is eighteen, is carrying a beach shoulder bag and a camera. Malcolm is carrying two tabloid newspapers and a paperback book. He is nearly seventeen. Both are dressed in casual beach-wear

Freda Good-morning, parents. Camped in the same old spot.

Jack That's right . . . in the same old spot. You've made your usual sweat to help, I see.

Freda We've been for the papers for you.

Jack And that takes two of you? It's not heavy reading.

Malcolm Dad, you've made a joke there, I think.

Jack And what have you been doing?

Malcolm Bought a book.

Jack Another book? You bought one just the other day.

Malcolm I've read it. Finished it yesterday.

Jack It's impossible for anyone to read a book as fast as you do. What have you bought now? (*He takes the book from Malcolm and reads the title, then returns the book without comment*)

Malcolm How would you suggest I spend my money?

Jack I'm saying nothing—nothing!

Beryl Let's enjoy the sun, while it shines.

Jack D'you know, Beryl, you say that every morning.

Beryl I know. It keeps the rain away.

Freda begins stripping. Underneath her clothes she is wearing a bikini. The others give the impression of hovering and circling the "camp" like large birds before landing. Malcolm puts the newspapers under Jack's sun-lounger and is the first to settle with his book on a towel. Beryl fusses and adjusts various items in the camp

Jack Don't touch anything—it's all set correctly.

Freda Mum, d'you have the sun-cream?

Beryl In the blue bag. It's a bit early for stripping off.

Freda I want to get the cream on before it gets too hot.

Jack (*to Freda*) Are you honouring us with your presence today? (*He sits on a sun-lounger*)

Freda Yes, I thought I might. (*She searches the bag*)

Beryl (*quickly*) That will be nice.

Freda For a while anyway.

Jack There was a time when we all stayed together on the beach. Do you remember that?

Freda There was a time when I wore black stockings and navy knickers.

Jack What is that supposed to mean?

Freda We're all getting older—growing up. (*She finds the cream*) Ah! (*To Jack*) Or haven't you noticed?

Jack I've noticed. (*He stares hard at Freda*)

Freda (*returning the stare*) Good! (*She begins rubbing her body with cream*)

Jack What exactly do you do at the other end of the beach?

Freda Nothing very much.

Jack Then what's the point of going there?

Freda To see my friends.

Jack All right! Why don't they come up this end of the beach sometimes, to see us?

Freda I guess they don't want to. All the action is that end. It's deadly dull here . . . Well, isn't it?

Jack I don't think so. I don't think so. Who are these friends? Are they on holiday?

Freda Some of them—some.

Jack What are the others—beach layabouts?

Freda I thought that's what you do on the beach—lay about.

Jack Don't be clever with me, my girl.
Freda (*after a pause*) Would you really like me to bring a friend here?
Jack Yes. Why shouldn't I?
Freda All right, I'll do that.
Jack Yes, do that.
Freda (*defiantly*) I will.

Jack reacts to the verbal encounter by leaping to his feet and picking up a beach ball

Jack Come on, Malcolm, let's have a game.

No response from Malcolm

   Malcolm!
Malcolm A bit later, eh, Dad?
Jack Hell! What's the matter with everybody?
Beryl I'll play a game with you.
Jack You'll do.
Beryl Thanks.
Jack Come on! (*He throws the ball at Beryl*)
Beryl (*catching it*) Not now. Later on. I've only just sat down.
Jack Women!

Beryl puts the ball away

   It's going to be hot today. The wind's——

Beryl
Freda   (*together*)—in the right direction.
Malcom
Jack

Beryl, Freda and Malcolm laugh. It's an old joke

Jack Funny!
Freda (*handing the sun-cream to Beryl*) Mum, rub some in my back.
Beryl (*with a slight grumble*) All right. Give it here.

Beryl takes the tube of cream from Freda and begins rubbing Freda's back. Malcolm continues reading. Jack stands peering into the distance. It is a kind of tableau

   I was thinking . . . I don't know what made me think of it. (*She pauses*)

Jack, Malcolm and Freda are attracted by the silence

Freda Come on then! What were you thinking?
Beryl I don't know how it came into my mind—but d'you remember, Jack—when these two were small—you used to take that old bugle on the beach?
Freda A bugle?
Jack Yes, I remember that.
Freda Whatever for?
Beryl Well, if you or Malcolm wandered off—when we were on the beach—your dad used to blow the bugle——

Freda That's not true!

Beryl —so that you'd know where we were—if we wanted you.

Freda Dad, is it?

Jack What?

Freda True?

Jack Of course it's true. It's a bugle I had when I was in the Boys' Brigade —as a kid.

Freda Malcolm, did you hear that?

Malcolm (*not looking up; mumbling*) What?

Freda We were summoned by a blast from a bugle.

Beryl Not just a blast. Your dad could play tunes.

Freda Tunes! It gets better. Mum, how embarrassing!

Beryl It was.

Jack It was not!

Beryl It was! But I don't think I cared.

Freda Jack Mercer entertains! The Seaside Show!

Jack That's enough!

Freda Touchy.

Jack (*ignoring the remark and re-examining the camp*) Well, that's all set up—everything in place. (*He stretches his arms above his head*) Ah! This is the life! (*He pauses*) I wonder what happened to that bugle? In the loft I bet.

Beryl completes rubbing suntan cream into Freda's back

Beryl There you are. That's you done on the back. I think I'll put some on.

Freda I have to finish myself first.

Beryl Hurry up then. (*She looks at her hands*) My hands are looking better, and they're so much softer.

Freda Were they getting rough?

Beryl Of course they were. You know that. It's working in that office of ours.

Freda Mum, you don't have to work in the office. Dad could pay somebody.

Beryl Somebody has to do it until he replaces Stanley.

Jack Which is not going to be easy. (*He sits on his lounger*)

The family settles down. Freda lies on her stomach on a lounger. Beryl commences applying suntan cream. Jack puts his sun-hat over his eyes— stretches and exhales—then drums his stomach with his hands

Where are the newspapers?

No-one reacts

Newspapers please. (*He pauses*) Is everybody deaf or lame?

Beryl (*calmly*) Get them yourself.

Jack (*grumbling*) Is there no rest. (*He sits up*) Malcolm, where are the papers?

Malcolm is lost in his book

Malcolm!

Malcom Um?

Jack Where are the newspapers? Newspapers!

Malcolm Um? Under your lounger.

Jack (*annoyed*) Thank you very much. (*He snatches a newspaper from underneath the lounger, then speaks to the "switched-off" Malcolm, lightheartedly*) Malcolm, why don't you get off your backside and dig a sand-castle or something? Life is slipping by—and you're missing so much. (*He opens up the newspaper and almost immediately drops it on to his lap and looks out to sea and into his memories*) And there were sand-castles, Beryl, d'you remember?

Beryl Remember what?

Jack The sand-castles—and those speedboats I used to dig and carve out of the sand—when those two were small, d'you remember, Beryl? Nearly full size they were. Best bit of sand building on the beach. D'you remember, Malcolm?

Malcolm (*not looking up*) Um?

Jack The boats I used to build in the sand—for you. You sat in them, using your spades for levers.

Malcolm (*uninterested*) Yes, I remember.

Jack Thought you would. When we left the beach you used to trample on it so that no other kid could play with it.

Beryl He never did that.

Jack Oh, yes he did.

Beryl It was you who did that.

Jack I never did.

Beryl Oh, yes you did. You didn't want any other father getting the credit for your work.

Jack Me?

Beryl You! You never said so at the time. But I knew . . .

Jack You're being stupid, girl. (*He reads his newspaper*)

There is silence

> *Maurice, Helen and Sarah enter. They are carrying the minimum of equipment. Maurice is carrying a tartan rug and a wood and canvas "director's" chair. Sarah, an attractive sixteen-year-old, is carrying a duffel bag, a book and a deflated air-bed. Helen, a woman in early middle age, is carrying a holdall. She is conservatively dressed for the beach—an expensive summer dress and stockings or tights with low-heeled sandals. They hesitate at the rear of the beach before moving down to stop on the far side of the wind-shields*

The Mercers are unaware of their intrusion

Beryl (*to Jack*) Your friend hasn't turned up yet.

Jack My friend?

Beryl The one you were telling me . . .

Jack Oh! . . . Him with the piece of wood. Well, he's hardly a friend. Didn't talk to him all that long. It was that piece of wood . . . Could I see the Taj Malah—or something like that—that's what he said.

Beryl He sounds like a nut-case to me.
Jack I wouldn't say that.
Malcolm (*without looking up*) It's the Taj Mahal.
Jack What is?
Malcolm In India.
Jack That's what I said.
Maurice Good-morning.

Jack and Beryl are startled

Jack Oh! Oh, it's you. (*He stands up and glances at Beryl*) As a matter of
fact we were just talking about you. Isn't that right, Beryl?
Beryl Oh, is this the—er . . .?
Jack The gentleman I met earlier . . .
Beryl That you met earlier . . . (*She struggles to her feet*)
Jack On the beach.
Beryl On the beach. Yes . . . (*She tails off*)

*Freda and Malcolm are only vaguely interested in the new arrivals. Malcolm
soon returns to his book*

Jack (*to Maurice*) You decided to come then?
Maurice Yes . . .
Jack This end of the beach.
Maurice I mentioned it to Helen—that you said this end of the beach was
better.
Jack Yes. We think so, don't we Beryl.
Beryl Yes . . .
Jack Quieter.

There is a pause

Maurice Oh, I'm sorry. This is my wife, Helen—and my daughter, Sarah.
Jack (*offering his hand to Helen*) Pleased to meet you.
Helen (*not offering her hand*) Good-morning.
Jack And you're Sarah.
Sarah (*politely*) That's right.
Jack Well now—this is my wife Beryl—my daughter Freda and my son
Malcolm. (*He gives Malcolm a kick with the side of his foot*)
Beryl Pleased to meet you.
Freda (*standing up*) Hello!
Malcolm (*with a glance*) Hi!
Jack We have—er—been keeping a place for you—over there. We spread
the towels, as you can see.
Maurice That's kind of you—isn't it, Helen.
Helen (*unenthusiastically*) Very.
Jack (*moving to lift the towels*) This is a good spot. We always pitch here
—don't we, Beryl.
Beryl Yes, that's right, we do.
Freda (*cynically*) Every day—after day—after day.

Beryl flips Freda with a towel

Jack We come here a lot.

The Adamsons begin unloading their equipment. A large tartan rug, a cushion and a deflated air-bed are the major items; in quantity and quality a complete contrast to the Mercers' equipment. Maurice begins spreading out the rug close to the Mercers' camp. Helen is not happy with this position

Helen Over here, Maurice. It's flatter here—much flatter. (*She indicates a position at a greater distance from the Mercer family*)

Maurice re-positions the rug and begins setting up. The Mercers settle down. Jack remains standing

(*To Maurice*) Did you bring the pump for the bed?
Maurice Pump?
Helen For the air-bed.
Maurice Oh, the inflator. You put it in the bag.
Helen No, I certainly did not put it in the bag.
Maurice But I told you . . .
Helen Told me, Maurice?
Maurice Asked you, then.
Helen I don't recall you asking me, Maurice.
Maurice But I did.
Helen (*maintaining her calm*) It's your job to pack that sort of thing, dear. I must have the air-bed. The sand feels so hard here. You'll have to go back to the hotel.
Maurice Oh, dear. Perhaps Sarah will go.
Sarah Yes, all right . . .
Helen No. Maurice, you can go.
Jack Now please, if I might nose in here. You can borrow ours with pleasure. We have a pump . . .
Beryl We have two as a matter of fact. (*She stands*)

Helen is surprised that Beryl can hear the conversation

Jack It's here somewhere. (*He begins looking*)
Helen That's quite all right, Mr——?
Jack The name's Mercer—but call me Jack.
Helen It's not really necessary for you to go to any trouble.
Jack It's no trouble—no trouble at all. I know it's here somewhere—we blow up the dinghy with it. Ah! Here it is. (*He crosses to give Maurice the pump*) Can you manage?
Maurice I believe it's a bigger one than ours.
Jack It's the biggest you can get—this one.
Helen Maurice, would you prefer to use ours?
Maurice I don't think so. I'll be all right with this. (*He examines the tube*) The end connection looks the same. (*He spreads out the air-bed*)
Jack They're all to a set pattern—British Standard.

Maurice begins to connect the tube to the air-bed. Helen and Sarah watch

(*Hovering*) That's been a good pump—that has.

Maurice I can see it has. (*He commences pumping; operating the foot pedal with his hand*)

Jack No—it's a foot pump. You don't use your hands.

Helen Maurice, surely you can see that?

Maurice Ours is a hand pump. (*He struggles to his feet and makes a feeble effort pumping with his foot*)

Jack Let me do it for you.

Beryl Jack'll do it.

Jack eases his way to the pump

Maurice I can do it . . . I'm sure I can.

Jack Please—please, I'm in the garage trade, you know. (*He eases Maurice away from the pump*) Like this. (*He begins to pump expertly with his foot*) You see? You see what I mean?

There is an embarrassing pause

Beryl I don't know why we're all stood here looking. (*To Helen*) Would you like to sit on our lounger till your bed's blown up?

Helen (*loftily*) No, I don't think so. Thank you for the offer—but I think not. I must spread the rugs out properly. Maurice! If you're not pumping, then you can help.

Maurice Yes, yes. (*To Jack*) Will you be all right?

Jack Don't worry about me. Good for the circulation.

Helen produces a smaller rug of hand-knitted squares. She lays it carefully on the sand, then tugs precisely at the edges of the large rug, issuing orders to Maurice and fussing and fidgeting to pass the time. Freda stands up

Freda (*to Beryl*) Well, Mum, I think I'll be going.

Beryl What already?

Freda Yes. There are things to do. All right?

Beryl (*understandingly*) With your friends at the other end of the beach, I suppose.

Freda Something like that.

Beryl Why don't you stay with us, this morning? Just for your dad's sake.

Freda If I go while he's pumping that thing—then there won't be any fuss. You've got new friends here now. You'll be all right.

Beryl Stay with us just for this morning. For me then. Will you stay for me?

Freda (*considering*) Well, all right. Just for a little while.

Beryl Good girl.

Jack (*pressing the air-bed*) It's getting near the right pressure. You see? Will you try it for comfort?

Maurice It looks fine—absolutely fine. (*He presses the air-bed*) Helen doesn't like it too hard——

Jack Good! Good! I'm pleased to hear that.

Maurice —do you, Helen. (*To Jack*) I must say it's extremely kind of you to . . .

Jack Say no more. I enjoyed the excercise. (*He winces, holds his chest and exhales*)
Maurice Is something the matter?
Jack No. No, I'm all right—really. (*Recovering*) I'm OK. Somebody walked over my grave, as my old grandmother used to say. I'll be getting back to bed now. Leave you in peace. (*He returns to his lounger*)

Beryl sits on the side of her lounger

Beryl What happened to you?
Jack Nothing.
Beryl Are you not well?
Jack I'm fine. Stop fussing.

The Mercer family settle once again. On the other side, Sarah spreads herself carefully on the tartan rug and begins reading her book. Helen moves to the air-bed and prods it. Jack watches

It's quite safe.
Helen I'm sure it is. (*She sinks cautiously on to the air-bed, then adjusts her position several times*)

Maurice is hovering

Come along, Maurice, sit down.
Maurice Yes, I will. Where's the *Telegraph*?
Helen In the bag.

Maurice fumbles in the bag

Jack Would you like the *Daily Mirror*?
Maurice No, thank you . . .
Helen (*quietly*) I don't think so.
Maurice Later perhaps. (*He re-positions his chair and sits*)
Jack Right!

Helen begins reading a book. Maurice opens his newspaper. Jack tries to read his newspaper—but fidgets

Maurice (*to Helen*) What d'you think of this spot? D'you like it?
Helen Yes, it's . . . nice. (*She looks about her*) Very nice.

Beryl catches her eye

Beryl All settled nicely?

Helen smiles weakly

Good!
Helen (*to Maurice*) I'm just a little disappointed with these friends of yours.
Maurice They're not my friends.
Helen They are not at all the way you described them.
Maurice Oh, I don't know—they seem all right to me.
Helen Just a little on the common side, I would have thought.

Maurice That may be so . . .
Helen It is so, dear.
Maurice I'm sure they're very nice people.
Helen Of course they're nice people. I didn't say otherwise. (*She returns to her book*) I'm just a little disappointed.

Maurice looks at Helen for a few seconds then, realizing the conversation is at an end, reads his newspaper

Jack (*to Beryl*) They're nice people. Don't you think so?
Beryl (*uncertainly*) Yes. I think she's a bit potty.
Jack Potty?
Beryl Stuck-up. Thinks she's somebody.
Jack I wouldn't say that.
Beryl Oh, I would. (*She puts on her sun-glasses, sits on her lounger with her feet up and lights a cigarette*)

Freda is lying on her lounger showing her already browned back to the sun. Malcolm continues reading. Jack places his newspaper on his lap and picks up his binoculars. He looks at the sea

Beryl What are you looking at?
Jack Nothing. Nothing in particular. Only the sea.

The Lights slowly fade to a Black-out

SCENE 2

The same. 11.30 a.m.

Maurice, Helen and Sarah are in the same positions and have only slightly changed their attitudes

Jack and Beryl are on their loungers. Jack is asleep and Beryl is reading a magazine. Malcolm continues to read his book. Freda has gone

There is a pause, during which time Maurice, Helen and Beryl fidget a little and slightly adjust their positions to relieve an ache or stiffness. At almost rhythmic intervals they look up and glance or stare in random directions, sometimes at passing or static points of interest, and at other times at nothing in particular. Jack wakes, regaining consciousness with a few grunts

Jack (*sitting up*) Ah! I've been asleep. (*He looks at his watch*) Eleven-thirty. (*Apologetically*) Not for very long—only ten minutes. (*Seeing Freda's empty lounger*) Where's Freda?
Beryl She's gone.
Jack Gone where?
Beryl To the other end. I suppose that's where . . .
Jack She crept off when I was asleep.
Beryl I don't think she crept off. She just got up and went.
Jack (*raising his voice*) That really is typical of her. She has no right to do that. No right at all.
Beryl She can do as she pleases.
Jack Not when I'm asleep.

Helen looks up

Beryl Jack, not so loud.
Jack Now, did she have to go?
Beryl Jack——
Jack I thought she was staying here—for at least the morning.
Beryl —don't make such a fuss.

There is a short pause. Helen returns to her book

Jack Who is she mixing with at the other end of the beach?
Beryl (*calmly*) I believe there's a group of them.
Jack Group?
Beryl Young people—I think.
Jack You've seen them?
Beryl Yes. Yes, I wandered along the beach the other day. I've seen her—with the others.
Jack What sort of people are they? Are they the kind of . . .? (*He stands up and shields his eyes, peering to the far end of the beach*)

Beryl I don't know. You can't tell what people are, can you? Everybody looks the same in swimsuits.

Jack Are there any other girls?

Beryl Yes, I think so—a couple. All very brown.

Jack Coloured?

Beryl Sunburned.

Jack They'll be the wrong people—mark my words. They'll be the wrong 'uns.

Beryl Jack, she's eighteen. She can do as she likes.

Jack And we are her family.

Beryl But we are not her age.

Jack (*sitting down*) We are losing our little girl, d'you know that?

Beryl She is not a little girl.

Jack (*more loudly*) She is! (*Softly*) To me she is.

Helen (*to Maurice*) They seem to be having trouble with their daughter. She's gone somewhere—and your friend appears to be extremely displeased about it.

Maurice continues reading

Maurice, did you hear what I said?

Maurice I'm sorry. What is it? (*He looks across at the Mercers*)

Beryl (*looking at Helen but speaking to Jack*) I think she's talking about us.

Helen It doesn't matter.

Jack (*to Beryl*) Who is?

Maurice (*to Helen*) If you say so.

Beryl She is. (*She raises her hand to perform a limp wave*)

Maurice acknowledges with a similar action

Helen (*to Maurice*) There's no reason why you should wave back. (*She returns to her book*)

Maurice Oh, I'm sorry.

Jack (*to Beryl*) What's she saying?

Beryl I've no idea. No idea . . . but she was talking about us.

There is a pause. The two families settle down again. Jack reads the paper. Beryl examines her feet

I don't know what they'll think of us. The top of my feet are sore.

Jack What d'you mean?

Beryl The sun has caught the top of my feet.

Jack No . . . "What they'll think of us," you said.

Beryl Well . . . what they'll think of you. Making all that fuss and noise.

Jack Noise! What noise?

Helen (*to Maurice*) They are rather—unusual people. Don't you think so, Maurice?

Maurice Friendly. I would say—friendly.

Helen (*sardonically*) Oh, very friendly. (*She pauses*) I've never seen so much beach equipment. They must have a lorry—or a horse to bring it to the beach.

Maurice No, I saw him. He carries most of it himself.

Helen That doesn't surprise me. He appears to be very versatile.

There is a pause. Maurice reads. Helen shields her eyes and examines the locale

It's a very pleasant spot—I'll grant you that—but I haven't seen any toilets.

Maurice Umm?

Helen I haven't seen any toilets.

Maurice Are you wanting to . . .?

Helen Not at the moment, but I shall be—very soon. You know what the sound of the sea does to me. We should have sat further back.

Maurice Shall I ask about the toilets?

Helen No. Certainly not. I can do that—if it becomes necessary.

Beryl (*to Jack*) Shall we have some coffee?

Jack Yes, that's what we'll do. Let's bloody well do something. (*He leaps up and from one of the containers, produces a flask*) Here we are! Catch! (*He pretends to throw*)

Beryl Don't be silly.

Jack (*handing her the flask*) Why not? If you can't be silly on your holiday, when can you be silly?

Beryl Got the cups?

Jack produces matching cups and a plastic tray

Jack Shall I pour?

Beryl No, I'll do it. (*She unscrews the cap from the flask and begins pouring*)

Helen gets up and views the landscape

Helen (*to Maurice*) I'm going for a walk. I shouldn't be very long.

She strolls away, carefully avoiding a glance in the Mercers' direction, and exits

Beryl (*to Jack*) Perhaps your friends would like a drink?

Jack Yes, why not. (*Calling to Maurice*) Excuse me. Would you like a drink? It's only coffee. Oh, has your wife gone somewhere?

Maurice Yes. Yes, she has—as a matter of fact.

Beryl Oh, dear. She could have had a cup.

Jack (*to Maurice*) You'll have one?

Maurice (*considering*) Thank you. Thank you very much.

Jack We always bring a couple of flasks . . . for elevenses.

Maurice Shall I come over?

Jack Yes, do that. Why not?

Maurice stands up and crosses, almost excitedly

Beryl Your daughter—will she have one?

Maurice Yes—I think so. (*Calling to Sarah*) Sarah!

Sarah and Malcolm look up, Malcolm to look only at Sarah

Would you like a cup of coffee?

Sarah (*hesitating*) No thank you.

Jack Are you sure? Plenty here.

Sarah Quite sure, thank you. (*She continues reading*)

Maurice She is always reading.

Jack (*snapping his fingers*) Snap! I have one of those. (*He points at Malcolm*)

Beryl Your wife's gone. Does she . . . ?

Maurice Yes—I believe she's looking for a toilet.

Beryl (*anxiously*) A toilet? She'll not find one at this end. (*She hands her cup and the flask to Jack*) Take this, Jack. (*She stands up*) Which way did she go? (*She shields her eyes and surveys*)

Maurice I really don't know . . . but . . .

Beryl Ah! There she is. I'll catch her and tell her she can use ours. Have you got the key, Jack?

Jack's hands are full with the cup and flask

Jack In my trousers pocket.

Beryl thrusts her hand into his trousers pocket

Careful what you're doing in there.

Beryl Why? Is there something valuable in there?

Jack I think so.

Beryl (*finding the key*) Here we are.

Beryl moves away and exits

Jack watches her exit, still holding the flask and cup

Jack (*to Maurice*) This cup of coffee will be cold. I'll have this one. Will you hold it?

Maurice That's all right—I'll drink it.

Jack (*firmly*) No! I'm saying you'll have a hot one. Right?

Maurice Sorry.

Jack pours another cup

Jack Sit down here, Maurice. It is Maurice . . . ?

Maurice (*sitting*) Yes.

Jack I heard your wife say . . .

Maurice Yes, that's right.

Jack I'm Jack. (*He sits on the edge of the lounger*) Let's swap cups.

They face each other and swap cups

Well—cheers then, Maurice!

Maurice Cheers!

They drink. There is a short pause

Jack Is everything OK? Have you settled into your camp?

Maurice Yes—fine. Fine. (*He pauses*) There is just one thing.

Jack Um?

Maurice Your wife took a key. Did she say it was for the toilet?

Jack (*amused*) No! That was the key to our caravan. She is going to let your wife use the toilet.

Maurice Oh! I didn't know you were in a caravan.

Jack Oh, yes. We're caravan people, we are . . . have been for years. (*He pauses*) You're not caravan people?

Maurice No. Helen said she would never stay in a caravan.

Jack Ah!

Maurice I never have, but I would like to try it.

Jack So you should. It's a good life. We use it weekends mostly. Convenient when you have a business. It means you can get away at short notice, and get back at short notice.

Maurice (*with a sudden spark of interest*) So you have your own business.

Jack Yes. Yes, I do.

Maurice In what field?

Jack Motor trade.

Maurice Really!

Jack Two garages—service stations and repairs. You know the sort of thing. Five miles apart . . . two good positions. It's very difficult to get away for a holiday.

Maurice That really is interesting.

Jack It's a bloody worry, I don't know about interesting. (*To Malcolm*) Malcolm, d'you want a drink?

Malcolm Is there any Coke? (*He raises his hand without looking up*)

Jack I expect so. Have a look.

Malcolm I will in a minute.

Jack Please yourself.

Malcolm I will.

Jack (*to Maurice*) What was I saying? Ah, yes—about the business and the worry. It's all the paperwork that kills my pleasure. It's no lie when I say that paperwork is more complicated to me than repairing the cars —and that's a fact.

Maurice But you have somebody handling that side of things.

Jack Yes—at least I did, but that's another problem. The fellow I had as office manager, Stanley—Stanley King, he left me a few weeks ago. He's taking over a pub, would you believe. Now that leaves two women, and a junior who does a bit of typing and switchboard.

Maurice That's very inconvenient for you.

Jack Too true, Maurice—too true. Beryl's been helping out, and I've been doing a bit at home—but I was not going to give up my holiday, oh no. What they can't handle I've told them to stick in the pending tray. You see, Maurice, I'm not a paperwork man.

Maurice I see . . .

Jack I started as a one-man business in an old warehouse in Millwall. I'm an engineer . . . that's what I am, and that's what I enjoy doing. But a business won't allow you to do what you enjoy. D'you see what I mean?

Maurice Yes, I do.
Jack And what do you do for a living then, Maurice?

Sarah looks up

Maurice (*hesitating*) I'm an accountant.
Jack (*impressed*) Are you really!
Maurice Yes, I . . .
Jack I'm impressed with that.
Maurice There's nothing impressive about it.
Jack I think there is. Clever people, accountants. They let others do the work, sweat and grind, while they sit at their desks and record the results—and sometimes manipulate them. Manipulators, that's what they are.
Maurice That's over-simplifying.
Jack I don't think so. I'm not being critical—don't think that—I pay an accountant a good fat cheque every year just to record the results of my grafting. I envy him—believe me.
Maurice There is a little more to it than that.
Jack Then you are some kind of special accountant?
Maurice (*hesitating, glancing at Sarah*) Well—no. I'm a financial director of a small company.
Jack Oh, that sounds much too important for me. I pass on that one.

They finish drinking their coffee. Jack places his cup on the plastic tray. Maurice does the same

Maurice I can assure you it is not that important. It's only a small company. Thank you for the coffee.
Jack Pleasure. My pleasure, Maurice. I do go on a bit when it comes to paperwork. No hard feelings?
Maurice Certainly not. I must get back to—my newspaper. (*He stands*) Thank you once again.
Jack You can stay here until the ladies come back. (*He stands*)
Maurice Very kind of you, but I think I'll go back, if it's all the same to you.
Jack It's all the same to me.

Maurice returns to his chair and picks up his newspaper. Jack wipes the cups with tissues and clears them away. Malcolm collects a Coke, walking lethargically to one of the bags and returning to sit on Jack's lounger

(*Suddenly raising his voice*) Hey! Maurice! Would you care for a game of Hash Bash?

Sarah and Malcolm, as well as Maurice, are startled

Maurice (*after a puzzled pause*) Hash Bash?
Jack Don't tell me you haven't played Hash Bash. Everybody plays it. (*He begins to search through the equipment*) I have the bat and shuttle-cock here somewhere. Here we are. (*He produces two wooden oversized*

table-tennis-type bats and a shuttlecock) We play this game all the time—
don't we, Malcolm?
Malcolm We play a bit.
Jack More than a bit. We play a hell of a lot.
Malcolm You play a lot—the rest of us play a little.
Maurice (*hesitating*) I'm not very good at beach games. Never have been.
Jack Rubbish! Everybody can play this—even Beryl. Mark you, she's
not very good—bottom of the family league. Please don't ask who's at
the top. (*He moves to Maurice*) Modesty forbids . . . (*He takes a swipe at
the shuttlecock and misses*)
Maurice Really, I don't think I should be very good at it.
Jack Then you will need some practice. (*He offers a bat to Maurice*)
Here you are.

Maurice takes the bat cautiously

We try to play games regularly around here. Stops other people en-
croaching on our patch. Stops them sitting too close. See what I mean?
Maurice Yes. Yes, I think I do. Like beating a boundary.
Jack Is it?
Maurice I think so . . . in a way.
Jack If you say so, Maurice. Come on, have a bash at Hash Bash.

Maurice considers for a moment

Maurice (*suddenly*) All right. (*He stands up and looks for Helen*) All
right . . . I will.
Jack Good! Great! Now stand somewhere there.

He positions Maurice and then himself a few yards away

I'll play against the wind . . . what there is of it. There's nothing to it.
Ready?
Maurice What is the object of the game?
Jack The object of the game? Ah, well—there is no real object. You must
hit the ball backwards and forwards—just try to keep it going. See
what I mean?
Maurice Is that all?
Jack "Is that all?" he says! It's not easy, I can tell you. Ready?
Maurice I can see it's not easy. Is there any scoring?
Jack No.
Maurice Good.
Jack Ready?
Maurice Rather more like a physical excercise—than a game.
Jack (*impatiently*) Yes. Are you ready?
Maurice I think so.

*The game commences—volleying the shuttlecock to each other. The duration
of the rallies are short. Jack plays energetically but his skill does not measure
up to his enthusiasm. Maurice is not such an accomplished player as Jack,
but makes up with economy of effort. When the shuttle falls to the sand,*

*which is often, Jack is quick to coach and advise. They are boys again.
Jack's excitement and enthusiasm finally result in him falling in an ungainly
manner to the ground in an effort to retrieve a wild return from Maurice. He
lies quite still on his back, breathing heavily, almost to the point of distress*

Are you all right?

*No immediate answer from Jack. He eventually sits up and briefly rubs his
chest hiding the effects of a slight pain*

Jack Yes, I'm all right. (*He struggles to his feet*) It's awkward playing on
this slope. Let's play somewhere over there. It's much flatter.
Maurice Are you all right?
Jack (*indignantly*) I'm all right—I'm all right. Don't make a fuss. I just
fell awkwardly here. Come on, it's much flatter over there.

He walks away. Maurice hesitates. Jack turns

Come on, Maurice. You're playing very well.
Maurice You think so?
Jack You're doing great.
Maurice I played a bit of tennis at the local club—Oxted.
Jack You live at Oxted?
Maurice Near to it.
Jack Then you're not far from us. We live at Croydon.
Maurice Well—what a coincidence.
Jack Ten or twelve miles from Oxted, no more. It's a small world. Come
on—let's play over there.

Jack moves away. Maurice looks thoughtfully at his bat, then slowly follows

They exit, Jack still mumbling about the smallness of the world

*Malcolm and Sarah continue reading. The performance by Maurice and
Jack has, until now, attracted brief glances from them. After a short pause,
Malcolm turns his head slowly to look at Sarah. Sarah senses this move and
responds in the same way. Their eyes meet and are held. After a few seconds
Malcolm begins to laugh—gently at first. Sarah's stored emotions are
apparently the same. She begins to laugh. Their laughter increases in volume
and intensity*

Malcolm (*through the laughter*) They really are so funny.
Sarah Yes . . .

Malcolm stands up and looks off at Jack and Maurice

Malcolm Not just those two—all of them. They are so ridiculous! Parents!
Sarah I know . . . I know . . .

The laughter begins to subside

Malcolm It's not really fair to laugh—but if you didn't, you'd have to cry.
They're more like kids than we are. They really are.

The laughter stops. Their gaze at each other is held for a few seconds

Sarah What are you reading?
Malcolm Thomas Hardy.
Sarah So am I.
Malcolm *The Mayor of Casterbridge.*
Sarah So am I.
Malcolm Really? (*He moves closer to Sarah*)
Sara (*showing the cover of her book*) There you are.
Malcolm What a coincidence. Don't you think so?
Sarah Yes.
Malcolm What d'you think of it?
Sarah I like it.
Malcolm So do I.

There is a short pause

Sarah Would you like to sit down?
Malcolm I don't think your mother would approve——

Sarah laughs

   —but I will. (*He sits next to Sarah*) I'll take the chance.
Sarah Have you been reading Hardy for O levels?
Malcolm Yes. And you?
Sarah Yes. Isn't that——
Malcolm ⎱
Sarah ⎰ (*together*)—incredible! (*They laugh*)
Malcolm I've got sand on your rug.
Sarah That's all right.
Malcolm From my legs. (*He stands up and brushes his legs*)
Sarah It doesn't matter.
Malcolm Sand gets everywhere. (*He settles again*)
Sarah Are you having a good holiday?
Malcolm Yes, at times. Are you?
Sarah We arrived only last night——
Malcolm Ah, yes.
Sarah —but I don't think I'm going to enjoy it.
Malcolm Why not?
Sarah (*hesitating*) Family problems—really.
Malcolm There are always family problems; at least there is in our family.
Sarah My mother's turning it into a bit of a crisis.
Malcolm My father usually manages to do that sort of thing. (*He pauses*)
   What other Hardy books have you read?
Sarah Oh . . . *Far from the Madding Crowd*—and *Tess*—for O level.
Malcolm Have you read *The Woodlanders*?
Sarah No. (*After a short pause*) Do you like his writing?
Malcolm Hardy? (*After a brief consideration*) Yes . . .
Sarah You're not sure.
Malcolm Yes, I'm sure . . . although I find his pessimism just . . . just a
   little too much, at times.

Sarah Really?

Malcolm I think so. Most of the people in the novels are . . . are seemingly trapped—hopelessly trapped one way or another . . . by their environment, mostly.

Sarah Well, yes . . . but there are always one or two characters who are trying to break out. There is some optimism—surely?

Malcolm (*considering*) There is some . . . some.

Sarah You're taking A-level English?

Malcolm If I'm allowed to go on. My father wants me to join him in the business.

Sarah Oh! What kind of business is that?

Malcolm Service stations—car repairs—garage. Whatever you like to call it.

Sarah That sounds interesting.

Malcolm Yes—but you see, I'm not in the least bit interested. I'm my father's big disappointment.

Sarah I suppose you can understand how he feels.

Malcolm Sure. Sure I can, but he doesn't try to understand how I feel.

Sarah You want to go on to university?

Malcolm Yes.

Sarah To what end?

Malcolm What do I want to do after university? No idea.

Sarah No idea?

Malcolm No. I just want to take English because I enjoy doing it. The process of learning is interesting enough for me—at present. What about you?

Sarah I want to get a degree—and then teach.

Malcolm Conventional.

Sarah Yes, it is—and why not?

Malcolm Why not indeed. (*He pauses*) The sea looks inviting.

They stare at the sea

Not many people in. (*He pauses*) D'you enjoy a swim?

Sarah Yes, if the water's warm.

Malcolm It's never warm here. What about now?

Sarah A swim? No, not now. (*She pauses*) Later perhaps.

Malcolm Then what about a walk?

Sarah (*considering*) Where to?

Malcolm (*considering*) That way—over the rocks. Too many people the other way.

Sarah (*hesitating*) All right.

Malcolm (*standing*) Better tell the paters. Are they still playing? (*He peers*) Yes, they are.

Sarah (*standing*) I shouldn't.

Malcolm Not so energetically. Shouldn't what?

Sarah Tell them.

Malcolm Just wander off?

Sarah Why not? Father will probably make a fuss because—Mummy's not here, and she most certainly would make a fuss if she were.

Malcolm Then we'll play Romeo and Juliet.

Sarah Something like that.

Malcolm Come along then. We won't take T. Hardy with us—three's a crowd.

They place their books close together on the rug then exit

Beryl and Helen appear at the rear of the beach. They are walking slowly, carrying a basket hamper between them. Beryl is talking to a disinterested Helen

Beryl (*coming into earshot*) . . . it really is a problem. I buy most of my food monthly. We go to the local supermarket, it's just about—well, no more than a couple of miles from the house, and very useful. Jack pays by cheque and we're all right then for a month or so—for food, that is. Saves a lot of time. Do you shop at a supermarket?

Helen Um? Supermarket! No . . . very rarely. I patronize the local shop. I like to have personal service.

Beryl Well, that's nice, if you have the time. Shall we put the hamper down here?

They place the hamper close to Beryl's lounger

Thank you for your help.

Helen Thank you for the use of your toilet.

Beryl My pleasure.

Helen No mine, I believe.

Beryl You'll be having lunch at your hotel?

Helen No. I have a few things in the bag. We never eat at lunch-time. Just a snack.

Beryl You're not full-board at the hotel?

Helen Half-board. (*She becomes aware of the fact that both camps are uninhabited*) Where is everyone?

Beryl (*equally surprised*) Oh, they've all gone.

Helen That's odd.

Beryl They can't be far away. (*She scans the beach*) There they are. Over there . . . Jack and—and your husband. They're playing a game. See?

Helen (*slightly annoyed*) So they are. Whatever for, I wonder. (*She takes a few strides up the beach and calls*) Maurice! Maurice! (*She beckons*)

Beryl They seem to be enjoying themselves. Playing Hash Bash.

Helen Hash . . . what? (*She gives Beryl a quick but distainful glance*)

Maurice and Jack enter. Both are puffing a little

Maurice (*to Helen*) We've been playing——

Helen glares

—Hash Bash. (*He looks at the bat, embarrassed, and hands it to Jack*) There you are.

Jack (*loudly to annoy Helen*) Thank you, Maurice.

Helen It sounds a ridiculous game. Where's Sarah?

Maurice Sarah? (*He looks at the empty rug*) I don't know.

Helen Didn't she say she was going?

Maurice No, I didn't see her go.

Helen Then everything has been left unattended.

Maurice We were just over there. (*He looks to Jack for support*)

Jack Not too far away.

Helen ignores Jack's remark

Beryl Malcolm seems to be missing as well. Perhaps they've gone off together.

Helen I doubt that very much. Let's see if there's anything missing. (*She crosses to the rug*) What's this? Two books. That's Sarah's . . . (*she picks up Malcolm's book*) . . . but this isn't hers. It's a paperback!

Beryl It must be Malcolm's.

Jack (*crossing*) Let me see. (*He takes the book from Helen*) Yes, that's his. I remember the picture on the front.

Helen It's the same book! *The Mayor of Casterbridge.* That's strange. Are they reading the same book?

Jack I don't think that's indecent, is it—reading the same book? (*He enjoys the joke alone*)

Helen I didn't say it was.

Maurice Have they gone somewhere together?

Beryl They could have.

Helen She said nothing to you, Maurice?

Maurice No.

Helen And you didn't see her go?

Maurice No.

Helen (*to Jack*) Did you see your son go?

Jack (*amused*) No, I didn't! Must there be an inquisition? Does it matter?

Helen It matters to me—where my daughter is.

Jack As I see it—your daughter was reading over there. Malcolm, my son, was reading over here. They're alone and they get chatting a bit. He went over there and sat with her—or she invited him over.

Helen Invited! Very unlikely . . .

Jack Or she invited him over. They talked about their books . . . got weary of sitting on their backsides and decided to go for a walk and quite frankly I'm glad he has. He's been sitting on his ass all the morning. Do him good to move about. It wouldn't do—what's-her-name—Sarah any harm either.

Helen She enjoys reading.

Beryl And so does my Malcolm.

Helen (*scanning the beach*) It's most unlike her to go anywhere without letting me know. I doubt very much that they're together.

Jack And why not?

Helen Shall we say, intuition—a feeling I have.

Jack (*lightly*) You think my son is an unlikely companion for your
    daughter?
Helen I didn't say that.
Jack I know you didn't say it, but I think that's what you meant.
Helen Well, of course, you can think what you like. (*She moves to her
    air-bed*) I just hope they are both being sensible.
Jack I'm not sure that I share your hopes.

Helen turns enquiringly

    Being sensible is often being dull.
Helen Is that your own homespun philosophy, Mr—ah——?
Jack It could be—yes. It could be.

*Maurice has remained with Jack and Beryl. Helen begins to settle on the
air-bed*

Maurice (*to Jack; quietly*) Helen really is a good sort, if you get to know
    her.
Jack I'm sure she is. (*To Beryl*) Beryl, you've brought the hamper down.
    How did you manage that?
Beryl Helen helped me.
Jack Helen! Oh, so it's Helen now. And this is my very good friend,
    Maurice. Isn't it, Maurice.
Maurice I will say this, Helen quite likes it here.
Jack Good, old son, good.
Helen Maurice!
Maurice Coming! (*To Jack*) Excuse me.
Jack And why not!

Jack allows Maurice to pass. Maurice joins Helen

Beryl (*to Jack*) What time are we having lunch?
Jack One o'clock—the usual time. We mustn't let missing children upset
    our routine.

Jack and Beryl settle on their loungers

Helen (*to Maurice*) Has Sarah gone with that son of theirs?
Maurice All I can say is that I didn't see them go.
Helen You were too busy playing silly games.
Maurice Hash Bash. I enjoyed it.
Helen Ridiculous.
Beryl (*to Jack*) Did you enjoy your game?
Jack Um?
Beryl With what's-his-name—Maurice.
Jack Yes. Mind you, he's not very good at it.
Maurice (*to Helen*) It's a good game.
Helen D'you think so?
Maurice I surprised him—I believe I did—with the quality of my game.
Helen That surprises me. (*She pauses*) Did you know they were staying in
    a caravan?

Maurice Yes, he told me.

Jack (*to Beryl*) He's pretty fit for his age. He must be in his late fifties.

Beryl (*glancing at Maurice*) He must be.

Jack I thought I was fit, but he kept me going. As a matter of fact, I got myself a bit puffed.

Helen (*to Maurice*) She insisted that I used the toilet.

Maurice In the caravan?

Helen In the caravan. As you know, I've never liked caravans. Now that I've been in one, I like them even less.

Beryl (*to Jack*) I think she liked the caravan.

Jack Who? . . . Mrs—Helen?

Maurice (*to Helen*) The toilet must be small.

Helen It is small.

Beryl (*to Jack*) She said it was very nice.

Jack She said it was very nice?

Beryl Yes. Convenient, compact, comfortable.

Helen (*to Maurice*) You really couldn't swing a cat around inside. How the four of them manage to exist in there, I don't know. The living conditions are almost indecent.

Jack (*to Beryl*) Maurice told me she didn't like caravans. Mind you, that doesn't surprise me.

Helen (*to Maurice*) I can see now why they spread out when they are on the beach. It must be such a relief for them.

Beryl (*to Jack*) She didn't say she didn't like caravans.

Jack Too polite.

Beryl Two faced.

There is a pause, Jack stands up and looks through his binoculars

Helen (*to Jack*) Are you looking for your son?

Jack No, I'm not as a matter of fact.

Helen (*to Maurice*) If Sarah's not back very soon, I shall—we shall—go looking for her.

Maurice I'm sure she's all right.

Helen You cannot be sure about a thing like that. (*She pauses*) You seem to be very friendly with him.

Maurice Jack? He's all right.

Helen Not our type at all.

Maurice They own two service stations.

Helen She told me. Do you believe that?

Maurice Yes, I do. Why not?

Helen He doesn't seem—well—I can imagine him in a garage mending cars—yes, but not running a business.

Maurice I believe he's having trouble in that direction.

Helen I'm not surprised.

Jack (*sitting down; to Beryl*) There's a lot of people at that end of the beach.

Beryl Could you see Freda?

Jack Freda?

Beryl That's who you were looking for.
Jack (*considering*) No.
Beryl Liar.
Helen (*to Maurice*) Did you tell him your profession?
Maurice I told him a lie, yes. I said I was a financial director.
Helen Which is true. That is your status.
Maurice That is what I was. I have now been sacked.
Beryl (*to Jack*) Maurice is a director of some company. She did say the
    name——
Jack Financial Director.
Beryl —of the company. The name of the company.
Jack He didn't say the name to me.
Beryl D'you know, it's completely gone. I've forgotten it.
Jack He's an accountant.
Beryl Yes, I know that. It was the name of the firm.
Helen (*to Maurice*) There's no shame in what's happened. No shame at
    all. You did the best for that firm and they will be the losers. What I do
    blame you for—is letting them walk all over you. That is where you
    failed.

*Maurice has heard all this before. He shapes to reply but thinks better of it.
The two families settle again*

   *Freda enters—she has replaced her sun-top. Arnold follows. Freda moves
   down to join Jack and Beryl. Arnold stands a little way off*

Freda Hello! Hello!
Beryl Freda, dear! You're back then!
Freda Yes, I'm back. Hello, Dad!—I said I would.
Helen (*to Maurice*) I see she's back—the daughter.
Jack To what do we owe this honour?
Freda You asked me to bring one of my friends to see you—so I have.
Jack (*standing up*) Where?
Freda Here he is. (*Beckoning to Arnold*) Come along.

*Beryl stands up. Arnold moves slowly down the beach towards the Mercers'
camp. Jack and Beryl react expressively but in silence*

Helen (*to Maurice*) Now who can this character be?
Jack (*incredulously*) That's—that's Arnold!
Freda (*lightly*) That's right.
Maurice (*to Helen*) That's Arnold.
Jack He's the deck-chair man!
Arnold Good-morning, sir. The vending of deck chairs is the way I earn a
    crust, yes, but . . .
Jack Beryl, didn't I tell you—eh—about the type of people . . .?
Maurice (*to Helen*) That's the poet fellow I was telling you about.
Helen Really?
Freda (*to Arnold*) This is my mum——

Arnold takes Beryl's hand

Helen He looks like a tramp.
Maurice He talked about this piece of wood.
Helen So you said.
Freda (*to Beryl*)—and this is Arnold.
Arnold Enchanté madame. (*He kisses her hand*)

Beryl allows the kiss then pulls her hand uneasily away

Jack (*to Freda*) Is this some kind of joke?
Freda How d'you mean?
Jack He's not one of your friends. This is Arnold—the deck-chair man.
You can't kid me, I know him. You're setting this up. Everybody knows
Arnold!
Arnold Not everyone, surely. I'm too modest to agree with that.
Freda (*hugging Arnold's arm*) Arnold is a very good friend. Is that right,
Arnold?
Arnold It is indeed.
Beryl (*simply*) But you have other friends, dear.
Freda Of course I do. There's a few of us who get together isn't there,
Arnold.
Arnold Yes, oh yes. We are a merry band, who play a merry tune.
Jack (*to himself*) My God!

There is a short, embarrassed pause

Well—um—it's been a pleasure meeting you—ah—Arnold. You'll be
wanting to get back to your chairs, I'm sure.
Arnold No. No, it's all right. Some people are standing in for me.
Jack Ah.
Freda Some of our friends.
Jack (*disappointed*) Good . . . good.
Freda You gather this is my dad.
Arnold I gathered. (*To Jack*) You say you know me, now you have the
better of me there. I'm sorry, but I don't remember you at all. Have we
met somewhere before?
Jack Yes. I had one of your deck chairs—last year—when we were here.
We sat at your end of the beach—one afternoon.
Arnold Just one chair?
Jack Two chairs!
Freda Arnold, sit down and talk to Dad.
Arnold Sit down? Is that permissible?
Freda You'd like that, wouldn't you, Dad?
Jack (*who doesn't like*) I'm sure Arnold must have other things to do.
Arnold Yes, I have—but they can wait. They can wait.
Freda Sit down here—on the lounger.
Arnold Thank you. That's very kind. (*He sits on the lounger*)

*Jack sits on his lounger with some reluctance. Beryl sits on her lounger.
Freda kneels on the sand at the feet of Arnold*

Maurice (*to Helen*) He really is an interesting person.

Helen So you have said. But I find it difficult to accept that he is a poet, if he's friendly with her—or them, if it comes to that.

Maurice Jack said he was the deck-chair man.

Helen Ah, now that would be more in keeping—a beach-chair man. They would have little in common with a poet, now would they? But even so, he does look interesting, in a rough sort of way.

Jack (*to Arnold*) I must say—d'you know . . . d'you know, I find your kind of person very . . . very interesting.

Arnold My kind of person?

Jack Yes. I find you—find them—very interesting.

Arnold Do you really!

Jack Interesting kind of people.

Arnold In what way?

Jack In what way? (*After a pause*) Well—what you're at, what you're doing, why you're doing it—that kind of thing, if you see what I mean.

Arnold Well—beach chairs. I'm hiring out beach chairs——

Jack I know that.

Arnold —on behalf of the local council. All day and every day—nine o'clock till six.

Jack Yes, I do know that. I know that.

Arnold Right.

Jack That's your job.

Arnold How I earn money.

Jack But what happens at the end of the summer—the end of the season? No deck chairs required.

Arnold Well you know what it is with the beach-chair trade at the end of the season, it all folds up.

Freda (*laughing*) D'you get that, Dad?

No reaction from Jack

It all folds up!

Beryl Oh, I see. (*She laughs*)

Freda I've heard him say that one before.

Arnold Freda, you must not give away trade secrets. My beach-chair patter must sound impromptu—like another one—(*he mimics a voice*): "Tell me young man, is there any deposit on the chairs?" (*In his normal voice*) "No, madam—they're all perfectly clean."

Beryl (*chuckling*) Oh, I say . . .

Jack picks up his newspaper

Freda (*laughing*) D'you hear that, Dad?

Jack (*coldly*) I did.

Freda A deposit.

Jack I heard it. Amusing. Very amusing. (*He looks at his newspaper*)

There is a pause

Arnold You have it very comfortable here—very comfortable indeed—all mod cons.

Freda Family tradition. Self-sufficient on the beach. Everything for everything, and everything in its place. Isn't that right, Dad?

Jack (*still staring at the newspaper but obviously listening*) That is correct.

Arnold It's all a bit like the camp of some medieval king—all colour and order.

Freda Is it really?

Arnold Well—something like that. In those days of course, aluminium was yet to be discovered.

Beryl That's true. Things must have been heavier to carry in those days. They must have had more than one pack-horse.

Arnold Pack-horse?

Beryl That's a kind of family joke.

Arnold Oh.

There is a pause. Their attention drifts slightly

Beryl Perhaps, Mr Arnold, you would like to stay with us for lunch?

Arnold Well now . . .

Freda That's a good idea. (*She stands up*)

Beryl We always have a picnic lunch. There's plenty of—plenty of everything. You're most welcome.

Freda Why not? Arnold, why not? Dad would like that—someone to talk to—wouldn't you, Dad?

Jack What about the deck chairs? Are you not in charge of the deck chairs?

Arnold The deck chairs are in good hands. (*He considers*) Thank you. I would like to stay—for lunch.

Beryl Good. That's very nice.

Beryl and Freda begin to prepare lunch. They set up the folding table, and produce matching plastic crockery, glasses, food and a bottle of wine from the bags

Arnold It was kind of you to invite me. This is very pleasant. Very pleasant indeed. (*He sits up and notices Maurice*) That's odd . . . I seem to know that man over there. I know his face.

Jack drops his paper and looks at Maurice

Jack That's—that's—his name is Maurice. You met him on the beach here, this morning.

Arnold Yes, that's right, so I did. That's right. He said his name was Maurice, I remember. A rather tired man.

At that moment, Maurice looks across

He's looking this way. (*He waves. To Maurice*) Hello!

Maurice Hello! (*To Helen*) He's recognized me.

Arnold (*standing up*) Hello! How are you?

Maurice climbs to his feet and moves towards the Mercer camp. Arnold meets him halfway. They shake hands

Nice to see you again. You made it to the beach.

Maurice Yes.

Arnold With the family.

Maurice Yes. That's my wife. My daughter has . . . She's not here at the moment.

Arnold Marvellous—marvellous. It's a lovely day for the beach.

Maurice Let me introduce—ah . . .

Arnold Sure—sure . . .

Maurice leads Arnold to Helen

Maurice Helen—this is—ah—Arnold. You know, I told you how . . .

Arnold (*full of charm*) Very pleased to meet you. (*He offers his hand*)

Helen (*taking it; guardedly*) My husband has spoken of you several times already this morning.

Arnold (*not releasing her hand*) And he has spoken to me—of you.

Helen Really!

Arnold Your interest in poetry—the arts generally, and—Gilbert and Sullivan—I believe.

Helen (*surprised*) Yes. Yes, that's right—I didn't realize . . .

Arnold Realize?

Helen That he told you all that.

Arnold's charm has dropped Helen's guard

Arnold Oh, most certainly he told me—and I remembered because my interests are similar.

Helen Really?

Arnold Yes.

Helen (*considering*) We were led to believe that you were, or are, the deck-chair man—on the beach?

Arnold That is true.

Maurice But you told me you were a poet.

Arnold That is also true.

Helen Ah, I see. How intriguing. You actually write poetry?

Arnold I do.

Helen Seriously?

Arnold Is there any other way of writing poetry? Well, I must return to—ah—to where I was, if you'll excuse me. I believe lunch is nearly ready. It's been a pleasure talking to you.

Freda (*calling*) Arnold.

Helen Yes, and to you. We may have the opportunity of talking to you again.

Arnold You will have the opportunity, I've no doubt. I'm always on the beach. (*He returns to the Mercers' camp*)

Freda (*to Arnold*) I'm surprised you talked to her, anyway.

Arnold I'll talk to anyone. Is there something wrong with her? (*He settles comfortably on the lounger*) My, this is comfortable—very comfortable indeed. How long is it before we eat lunch?

Jack drops his paper on to his chest and stares at Arnold. The Lights slowly fade to a Black-out

SCENE 3

The same. 2.30 p.m.

Each camp has finished lunch. Jack and Beryl are positioned on their loungers, reading. Helen is sitting on her air-bed. Freda and Maurice have gone. A significant move has been made by Arnold. He now sits on the rug beside Helen. They are talking and, for the first time, we see Helen smile

Arnold (*to Helen*) . . . and at the top of the High Street one reaches the highest part of the old town. It's there the visitor will find the Parish Church. Are you interested in churches?

Helen Yes, I am.

Arnold Are you beginning to find all this local history chat a bit of a bore?

Helen Certainly not. I invited you to tell me. Please carry on. (*Almost imploringly*) Please.

Arnold Where was I?

Helen The Parish Church. You see, I was listening. (*She is delicately eating a shortbread biscuit*)

Arnold Ah, yes. The present church is mainly fifteenth century. There is a Norman window near the porch. The font is part Norman. Some bench ends are probably Norman. Some restoration work to the Chancel and Nave in the late nineteenth century. (*After a short pause*) Well, I think that's all I can tell you about the town.

Helen Thank you. Thank you very much. That was most informative. I shall make a point of exploring the old part of the town.

Arnold Yes, do that. You'll find some of it quite interesting.

Helen Would you care for a shortbread biscuit?

Arnold God, no thank you. I've eaten far too much for lunch over there— (*he indicates the Mercers' camp*)—with our friends. I have never seen so much provision in one hamper.

Helen They appear to do everything in rather a—big way.

Arnold Are they not friends of yours?

Helen Friends! Good heavens, no. They are, most certainly, not friends of mine. We have been acquainted with them since ten o'clock this morning —although on reflection, it does seem . . .

Arnold Longer?

Helen Longer. (*She smiles*) Yes. (*After a short pause*) All the evidence points to the fact that my daughter and their son have gone for a walk together.

Arnold Yes, I did glean that information from the encampment over there.

Helen Encampment?

Arnold indicates the Mercer family with a nod of his head

Oh. My husband has gone to look for them.

Arnold In which direction?

Helen (*standing up*) I've no idea . . . and I doubt, very much, if he has. (*She peers along the beach*) I know the main part of the town is that way, but what lies in that direction—(*she indicates*)—beyond the beach?

Arnold (*standing up*) Well—you can see the beach finishes just there. Beyond that point there are some rocks—no more sand . . . a few rocky inlets. There is local talk that two mermaids have, in the past, occupied that stretch of coast.

Helen Really.

Arnold The rocks sweep their way to the western headland, out there. (*He points*) On warm, clear summer evenings, the sun setting behind that western point is a sight never to be forgotten.

Helen Most of your descriptions tend to sound like excerpts from a guidebook.

Arnold That is exactly what they are.

Helen Really? Have you memorized them?

Arnold No, I wrote them.

Helen You wrote them!

Arnold I wrote this year's guidebook, yes.

Helen My, how clever.

Arnold Hardly clever. Let's not get carried away. It's mostly a crib from last year's book—with variations. It was something of a chore, but the money was most useful.

Helen Nevertheless someone had to do it—and that someone was you.

Arnold And that someone was me—I know, I know.

Helen So it is correct to say that you are a writer.

Arnold Ah. (*He considers*) Yes—and—no. Yes, I consider myself to be a writer—and no—no-one else has ever considered it.

Helen You've had nothing published?

Arnold Nothing—apart from the guidebook. Oh—and a slim volume of poems, that I published myself and paid for the printing—therefore it is for me to do the selling.

Helen Do you have a copy with you?

Arnold Yes—somewhere in the depth of this clothing.

Helen May I see it?

Arnold searches a few pockets before finding a thin, well-thumbed, volume of poems

Arnold There you are.

Helen May I?

Arnold hands the book to Helen. She sits in the chair and begins to examine the pages

Freda enters and joins Jack and Beryl. Freda has changed her sun-wear. She flops on to the lounger

Freda (*to Jack*) Here's the key to the caravan.

Jack (*taking the key*) Is everything all right in the van?

Freda Yes, I think so. What's Arnold doing over there?
Beryl He's left us to join Madam.
Freda Why?
Jack God knows why! I mean—they've nothing in common.
Freda She's old enough to be his mother.
Beryl I wouldn't say that.
Freda Well, I would.
Beryl He's getting on a bit.
Jack Twice your age I would say.
Freda So what?

There is a short pause

Jack Now he's out of the way, I'd like to know how you met up with him?
Freda One of the girls knew him from last year. Everybody knows Arnold
   —you said that.
Beryl There are younger boys. I've seen you with them on the beach.
Freda Of course there are.
Jack Just remember that you went to a good class of school—and I've
   paid for you to go to college—to learn a trade.
Freda It's an art, Dad, not a trade. I've told you that before . . . hair-
   dressing is an art.
Jack Whatever it is, you've learnt it, and I want you to make something
   of it—not messing about with the likes of him.
Freda He really is very intelligent—and very clever.
Jack Clever! Is that why he's in the deck-chair business—because he's
   clever?
Freda He has to earn money. He's really an artist . . . and a writer.
Jack Who says so?
Freda He says so.
Jack He's just a layabout.
Freda He is not.
Jack You're wasting this holiday away, my girl.
Freda I don't think so.
Beryl (*interceding*) What kind of things does he write, dear?
Freda I'm not sure. Poems—I think.
Jack (*aghast*) Poems?

During the following dialogue Freda sulks and reads

Helen (*to Arnold*) Although the book is rather small, you must find it
   gratifying to see your work in print.
Arnold Not very gratifying—when you consider I had it printed myself.
Helen Are you hoping to make money from it?
Arnold Not really. But I hope to cover the cost of the printing.
Helen Well, I most certainly will purchase a copy from you. (*She stands up*)
Arnold Thank you. Thank you very much. I have some copies in my hut
   on the beach. I'll get one for you.
Helen How much are they?

Arnold The price is on the back.

Helen (*looking at the back*) Well that's cheap enough. (*She takes a note from her handbag and gives it to Arnold*) There.

Arnold (*feeling in his pocket*) I'll give you the change.

Helen You can keep the change.

Arnold Are you sure?

Helen I'm sure.

Arnold Thank you. That will keep the wolf from the door for one more day.

Helen (*amused*) I'm sure it will. Are you married?

Arnold Why do you ask?

Helen Curiosity?

Arnold Curious about what?

Helen I am curious to know how a person, such as yourself, gets himself into such a . . . situation—or a way of life, as yours is?

Arnold That's easy—by choice.

Helen (*after a short pause*) You see, I know a little about it. I have a nephew who decided to be a—drop-out, is it? I believe that's the word.

Arnold Dear lady, I have not dropped out.

Helen (*smiling*) But you see, I have been talking to you for half an hour—and it doesn't take a genius to know that you are an intelligent person . . .

Arnold (*calmly*) Drop-outs are not necessarily unintelligent. I am not a drop-out.

Helen I'm sorry. I shouldn't pry.

Arnold That's all right—I deliberately and intentionally invite curiosity. It's part of my trade.

Helen Trade? Exactly, what are you?

Arnold (*considering*) I am, what I like to call, a professional character.

Helen And what is a professional character?

Arnold That is yet another question. (*He pauses*) Would you care to buy two of my books?

Helen Two books? Why?

Arnold Well you see, in most of the pubs in the town I can tell my story in return for a few drinks and a bite to eat. Two books could be the price of your curiosity.

Helen That's extortion.

Arnold No . . . it's trading.

Helen (*considering*) All right. Two books. (*She picks up her handbag*)

Arnold (*stopping her*) Please don't mar the moment with money. (*He pauses*) All right—your question. Am I married? I am not married—but I was.

Helen I see.

Arnold At least two lifetimes ago I was teaching art at a comprehensive school in Bristol—four years ago actually. I gave it up to come here to paint—seriously—which is the only way to paint. My wife was to follow when I had settled in. (*He pauses*) She never did.

Helen Ah . . .

Arnold She never did. She is a teacher—or was a teacher then—and has now married the head of the science department . . . very grand.

Helen I see . . .

Arnold Can't really blame her for that. (*He pauses*) Now that is when I put on my old straw hat—purchased at a church jumble sale—and moved into deck-chair vending, on behalf of the local council. In no time at all—quite unintentionally—I discovered that I was becoming a character—a talking point—a subject of conversation.

Helen Who? Who was talking?

Arnold The public at large—and holidaymakers in particular. So I made use of the situation. I worked at it—developed it a bit and became a professional character. "Everybody knows Arnold!" That's what they say. He has little trouble selling his paintings. They buy him drinks—they buy him food—and a few discerning people buy his book.

Helen Isn't that cheating?

Arnold It's a profession. I'm an entertainer. (*He begins to move away*)

Helen Just one moment.

Arnold (*stopping*) Yes?

Helen Is that story true?

Arnold Truth! You said nothing about truth! Truth would be three books. (*He moves away and begins to circle the beach—but is halted by the following dialogue*)

Maurice enters and joins Helen

Maurice (*to Helen*) No success I'm afraid.

Helen You haven't found her?

Maurice No.

Helen (*to Maurice*) The situation is becoming very serious. (*She addresses Jack from a distance*) I'm saying that it's becoming serious.

Jack I'm sorry—are you speaking to me?

Helen I'm addressing you, yes. Your son and my daughter have not yet returned. It is nearly three o'clock. Do you intend doing anything about it?

Jack No, I don't think so. (*He stands up*)

Helen Well, I must say, I'm surprised at your attitude.

Jack What is there to do?

Helen Go out and look for them. They've had no lunch.

Jack But they're not kids any more, are they. I don't know about you, but when we're back home, we don't spend all our time wondering where Malcolm is and what he's at. If I don't do it at home, then I'm certainly not bothering on holiday.

Helen Ridiculous . . .

Arnold sits on the sand, Freda joins him

Jack Sit down and relax.

Helen A most irresponsible attitude, I must say. My husband has been looking——

Jack I know that. Well done, Maurice!

Helen —and he's not seen a sign of them.

Jack (*almost kindly*) If you're that concerned, why don't you have a look for yourself?

Helen I shall do exactly that.

Jack Good for you.

Helen Maurice, you stay here. I shall go this way. (*She indicates the direction of the rocks*) Stay here . . . until I return.

Maurice Yes, I'll do that.

Jack You'll find it's all rocks in that direction.

Helen I can cope with rocks.

Jack And pools.

Helen And pools . . . and fools, if it comes to that.

Helen exits

Maurice hovers, then sits wearily in the chair

Freda (*to Arnold*) Here, what was that book you were showing her?

Arnold A book of poems.

Freda Your poems?

Arnold Yes.

Freda You've never shown it to me.

Arnold You've never asked, my dear. You've never asked.

Jack looks in the direction of Helen's exit. Beryl stands up and surveys the beach

Jack She's wasting her time going that way.

Beryl D'you think so?

Jack I know so.

Freda (*to Arnold*) Shall we have a look for our Malcolm?

Arnold "Our Malcolm"? "Shall we look for Malcolm?"—is that what you mean?

Freda That's what I mean, yes. I thought that's what I said.

Arnold, ignoring Freda's enquiring look, stares at the sea

Beryl Jack, it is a long time.

Jack What is?

Beryl Malcolm—and that girl. They've been away—it must be more than two hours.

Jack Stop worrying. To be honest with you, I'm more than relieved.

Beryl Why? How d'you mean, relieved?

Jack Well, he spends hours with his nose in those books. I was beginning to worry—just a bit. Wondering if he had the urge—you know—with girls.

Beryl Jack!

Jack Well, there's so many—you know—about today, you begin to wonder. At least he seems to be normal—which pleases me no end, I can tell you.

Beryl I think I shall go and look for them.

Scene 3

Jack They'll be all right.

Beryl I'm getting a little concerned. What are you going to do, Freda?

Freda Arnold, shall we go back along the beach and look for them?

Arnold (*still gazing*) Why not?

Freda We can pick up the others and have a look in the town. They may be in the town.

Arnold Let's do that. (*He stands up and moves off*)

Freda follows like a faithful dog

Freda Wait for me!

Arnold and Freda exit

There is a pause

Jack (*reflectively*) Beryl, d'you know this is the end of an era. This is the last holiday for us as a family . . . a family complete.

Beryl No, I don't think it is, Jack.

Jack I know it is. Everything is just drifting away, and becoming empty. We have brought both of them on holiday, year after year after year. Played in the sea—dug in the sand, spades, buckets, castles, wet costumes, seaweed—it's all gone, and I don't remember it going. Last year was our last family holiday—and d'you know we didn't realize it at the time.

Beryl But, you see, we've done it all—and we have the pleasure of remembering. We're lucky—we're lucky. You can't hang on to the past. Anyway, they're still our kids. Cheer up—you're being an old softy.

Jack (*angrily*) I am not! (*Softly*) It hurts!

There is a tense pause

Beryl (*gently*) I'm going to look for Malcolm . . . towards the caravan. Around that way. All right?

Jack is too lost to reply

Beryl exits

Jack and Maurice are alone

Jack (*at length*) Maurice, you're looking tired.

Maurice Yes. Yes, I am a little weary.

Jack It's not worth it, old son. Nothing's worth it. Come over here and have a rest on the lounger. Do you good—relax. (*He sits on the lounger*)

Maurice hesitates

Come on. (*He taps Beryl's lounger*)

Maurice hesitates then crosses

Stop worrying. Those two young people, take it from me, they'll be all right.

Maurice I'm not worrying. Sarah's a sensible girl. It's Helen who worries.

Jack Then let her do your worrying for you. Put your feet up—on the lounger—relax. We're all supposed to be on holiday and everybody is all tensed up, including me.

Maurice (*sitting on the louger*) I would have thought you to be a most relaxed person.

Jack Funny you should say that, Maurice, normally I am a relaxed person. People may not think so, but I am. Yet at this moment in time, I am really tensed up—piled up inside—on holiday! Can you believe that?

Maurice Yes, I can believe that. (*He pauses*) Would you mind very much, Jack, if I told you something? You don't mind if I call you Jack?

Jack That's my name.

Maurice (*after a short pause, searching for words*) You must try to understand Helen. She has her problems. You see—I'm going through a rather difficult time myself.

Jack Oh, I'm sorry to hear that.

There is a pause—Jack waits

Maurice It's not a situation I like talking about—you understand.

Jack And yet it would do you the world of good if you did.

Maurice You think so?

Jack I don't know, I just said that. Sometimes it helps. But I'm a good listener.

Maurice You see . . . I did say to you . . . (*He swings his feet on the lounger*)

Jack Yes?

Maurice I did say to you . . . that I was a financial director of a small company.

Jack Yes, you did say that.

Maurice Well—that, in fact, was a lie.

Jack Oh?

Maurice A white lie. A slight distortion of the truth.

Jack Ah!

Maurice You see I have, quite recently, been voted off the board of directors. Not for any malpractice, I hasten to add.

Jack Accepted.

Maurice waits for a question

What happened?

Maurice I've been a member of the board for twenty years.

Jack That's a long time.

Maurice Twenty years. It's a family-controlled firm and I helped the old man make it grow—slowly, but it grew—on a solid financial footing. Now he has died—and the two sons have taken control.

Jack I see the picture—I see it.

Maurice I'm not progressive enough—that's what they said—too cautious, which in a way is true—I admit to that. But that is the way of an accountant. Do you see what I mean?

Jack Maurice, accountants are a breed apart. If you've given this firm twenty years of your life—then surely they've seen you all right—eh? You've consulted your solicitor? You have the rights of a minority—you know that.

Maurice Oh, yes. They have been very fair financially. I have been adequately treated.

Jack Good!

Maurice (*his voice beginning to falter*) But that's not—well it's not everything, is it.

Jack No, that's not everything, but it's something.

Maurice (*beginning to cry*) It's the indignity. Do you understand that? The indignity of such a situation.

Jack Yes, I do understand that.

Maurice Helen is more concerned on that point than I am.

Jack I can imagine.

Maurice But there is always the indignity. I have a clear conscience. I have been a loyal servant. (*He pauses*) But where can I get another position at my age? I ask myself that question and there is no answer.

Jack I wouldn't say that. There's always an answer to every question. (*After a short pause*) Do you have to get another job—financially speaking? You don't have to answer that if . . .

Maurice is recovering

Maurice (*considering the answer*) Yes, I think I do. If we are to maintain our present standard of living—and give Sarah a good start, then I will have to find an income from somewhere.

Jack Your wife obviously wants to maintain your present standard.

Maurice Oh yes, and so do I. I'm not ready to be tossed on the tip for has-beens—not yet.

Jack Good for you, old son! Fighting talk! Now lie down and relax, you're on holiday. We're all on bloody holiday and we're getting uptight again. (*He produces a flask*) Here, have a nip of this whisky. I keep it for emergencies.

Maurice Well, I don't know . . .

Jack Go on.

Maurice Is it an emergency?

Jack Not really—but have some.

Maurice receives the flask and takes an ample swig

Maurice Helen thought we needed a holiday—to get away from . . . well, you know.

Jack I know, I know.

They both stretch out on the loungers

Maurice I'm sorry you had to listen to my problems.

Jack That's all right.

He glances sideways, in time to see Maurice take another long swig at the flask

Heh! Heh! Leave some for me.

Maurice Sorry. (*He returns the flask*)

Jack There may be a real emergency. (*He pauses*) Look at that sky—it's a perfect blue. (*He pauses; then aggressively*) Are you looking at the sky, Maurice?

Maurice Yes. Yes, I am.

Jack Good. (*He pauses for thought*) Maurice, you and I are at the crossroads.

Maurice Is that so?

Jack That is so.

Maurice I'm aware that I am. I wasn't aware that you . . .

Jack And so am I. (*After a short pause*) And so am I. (*He pauses*) Can you hear the sea?

Maurice (*lifting his head*) Yes. Yes, I can.

Jack Very persistent—very persistent the sea is. It never gives up. (*He pauses*) D'you know, often I lie on my back and watch the sky—and listen to the sea. Through all the years—when everything around us has been changing—the sea and the sky have stayed the same. Have you considered that?

Maurice No.

Jack As a kid, I'd lie down on the beach—usually in a hole I'd dug—and I'd watch the sky, and the clouds sailing past. Now the sensation is exactly the same . . . it hasn't changed. Relaxing . . . a good position for thinking.

They remain quite still, watching the sky and listening to the sea

Maurice?

No reply

Maurice?

Maurice Yes?

Jack I'm going to ask you something.

Maurice begins to move

Stay where you are.

Maurice What is it?

Jack This may sound silly to you at first—but how would you like to work for me?

Maurice (*raising his head*) Work for you?

Jack That's what I said.

Maurice What could I do, working for you?

Jack (*sitting up suddenly*) You could run my office and paperwork. (*Improvizing*) Organize the typist and clerk . . . do the wages and take over the work I pay my accountant to do. Tax returns and so on—and so on. You could do all that, right?

Maurice (*sitting up*) Well . . .

Jack What d'you think? (*He stands up*)

Maurice I'm too confused to think.

Jack Why? It's a straightforward enough offer—at least, I thought it was.

Maurice You can't make a proposition like that—to me. You don't really know me. You don't know my qualifications—or—or my capabilities.

Jack Of course, it wouldn't be such a high-flying job as the one you're used to, I realize that.

Maurice That's not important . . . I'm not concerned . . . You just can't make a proposition out of the blue, just like that.

Jack I can do as I please. I make most of my decisions that way—rightly or wrongly. You may say wrongly.

Maurice I really don't know what to say.

Jack (*lightly*) Would you like me to give you a formal interview—on the beach here? (*Mimicking*) "Good morning, Mr . . . ah . . . Mr—— please take a lounger. Can you tell me your reason for applying for this position? What has been your past experience? Umm?" Formal interviews, in my opinion, are a waste of time. I just ask myself, "Do I want this fellow working for me?" As simple as that. I tell him the job he has to do, and if he says he can do it, I give him the job. If he can't do it, then I'm afraid he has to go. So we won't bother with an interview. I wouldn't know what to ask you anyway—I've never interviewed an accountant.

Maurice Are you being serious?

Jack Of course I'm serious. I'm not doing this as a favour to you—don't get that idea. I'm doing myself a favour here. I need somebody to arrange what I call paperwork—it's that simple.

Maurice (*considering*) I must say it's kind of you to consider me for the position.

Jack If you want time to think—then take time—but not too long. You live—what, no more than ten miles away from my main garage. That's no distance in a car.

Maurice That's true. It would be no distance to travel.

Beryl enters

Beryl Here we are. (*She moves down*) There's no sign of Malcolm.

Maurice (*getting to his feet*) I'm sorry. I'm on your lounger.

Beryl That's all right, really. What's been going on here?

Jack Maurice and I have been having a serious chat. (*He stands up*)

Beryl Oh, that's nice.

Jack Well, not too serious. I'm trying to persuade him to come and work for us.

Beryl (*slightly concerned*) Really?

Jack Really.

Beryl That's interesting.

Jack Maurice can handle all our paperwork—accounts—tax—the lot.

Beryl (*to Maurice*) Are you not happy with the job that you have, Mr . . . ah——?

Jack He's looking around for somewhere different. Is that right, Maurice?

Maurice Yes . . . yes, that's right. I'm afraid your husband has made this offer straight off the cuff—with little thought. I'm not sure that he is serious.

Beryl (*with warmth*) Oh, he's serious. That's just how he is. That's how he's always been—when it comes to decisions. (*She looks along the beach*) I wonder where those children are?

Jack (*tapping Maurice on the back*) You see! There you are! Think it over. We'll have another chat later on.

Maurice I do need time to think—if you don't mind. Perhaps mention it to Helen . . .

Jack Well . . . (*He shrugs*)

Maurice Perhaps you'll excuse me? I'm sure you'll want to talk together.

Jack You don't have to go.

Maurice drifts back to the safety of his chair

Beryl (*to Jack*) I'm getting worried about those children.

Jack You're sounding like Helen. (*He sits on the lounger*) They'll be back when they're hungry. Stop worrying.

Beryl (*sitting on the lounger*) I hope you're right.

There is a pause

Jack It's getting very hot.

Beryl The best day we've had—as far as the weather goes. (*She looks at Maurice*)

Jack (*reading her thoughts*) Maurice could be just the sort of chap we want—reliable.

Beryl As long as you know what you're doing.

Jack He badly needs a job.

Beryl I guessed that. Is he out of work?

Jack Shall we say—early retirement.

Beryl I've never questioned your decisions.

Jack (*lightly*) Are you going to now?

Beryl No. But she'll never agree, of course.

Jack She may have to. (*He stands up and adjusts a piece of beach equipment*) I think I'll go for a walk. (*He stretches his arms and moves away. To Maurice*) Just going to stretch my legs.

Maurice acknowledges with a languish lift of the hand

Jack exits

There is a pause. Maurice sits with his head hanging in thought. Beryl stares at the sea. After digesting her thoughts, she looks across at Maurice

Beryl Maurice . . .

Maurice (*drawn back from his thoughts*) Um?

Beryl (*deeply felt*) My husband may seem brash, but he is in fact, a very kind man . . . very sincere and always—always honest.

Maurice (*after a short pause*) Thank you. Thank you very much for telling me that.

The Lights slowly fade to a Black-out

SCENE 4

The same. 4.30 p.m.

Beryl is alone, sitting on a lounger. She is repairing her make-up with the aid of a small hand mirror. Completing the task, she packs her beauty aids into a make-up bag, and primps her hair

> *Helen enters. She has been hurrying*

Beryl Oh, there you are.

Helen Where's my husband?

Beryl I believe he's gone to look for you.

Helen In which direction?

Beryl I've no idea. He just asked me to keep an eye on things. Is there something wrong?

Helen There most certainly is something wrong.

Beryl (*standing up*) Something's happened to the children. You've found them. What is it?

Helen What is it? I think disgusting would be an appropriate word.

Beryl What d'you mean by that? What's disgusting?

Helen Their behaviour.

Beryl Oh?

Helen Yes, oh! I have walked and scrambled over rocks for I don't know how far and I eventually found them swimming. Swimming off some rocks—without clothes on.

Beryl In the nude? I don't believe that.

Helen I am not blind. I saw them.

Beryl Not my Malcolm.

Helen Oh yes, your Malcolm. Both of them—together.

Beryl Malcolm has never done a thing like that before.

Helen Neither has Sarah. She is not that kind of girl. She would have to be persuaded to do such a thing.

Beryl What d'you mean by that?

Helen Persuaded—that's what I mean.

Beryl If you're saying that my Malcolm has led her on to do this, then I would say the boot was on the other foot.

Helen Don't be so ridiculous.

Beryl That is the kind of thing your sort of people do.

Helen What is?

Beryl Nude bathing. That's a middle-class pastime.

Helen What has middle-class to do with it?

Beryl Everything I would say. No morals. The middle class have no morals.

> *Maurice and Jack enter. Jack has now replaced his shorts with lightweight trousers*

Jack I met Maurice on the cliff path. (*To Helen*) We saw you coming back.

Helen Maurice, this woman is questioning our morals.

Maurice Oh?

Beryl "Woman"? What d'you mean exactly—"this woman"?

Jack Wait a minute! Wait a minute! What's happened here? What is it?

Beryl She says she's seen Malcolm and—and . . .

Helen I've seen your son and my daughter swimming—without clothes on.

Beryl In the nude.

Helen Not a stitch.

Jack Oh? (*After a short pause*) Where?

Helen Does it matter, where?

Jack Not really. Does it matter about them swimming in the nude?

Helen It certainly does matter. Does it not matter to you?

Jack No, it doesn't bother me too much.

Beryl Jack!

Helen Well, that just about says it all. Like father, like son.

Jack How d'you know they were in the nuddy? Did you see them get in the water—out of the water?

Helen I could see them from where I was standing. They were swimming—I was looking down. The water is very clear—and their clothes were piled on a rock. Your son refused to get out until I had left. (*To Maurice*) And Sarah did the same.

Maurice Refused to get out?

Helen Yes. But I had no wish to stay.

Jack Embarrassing?

Helen I told them to get dressed and return here immediately.

Jack (*after a short pause*) D'you know, it's something I've always wanted to do—swim in the nude. They say it's a marvellous feeling.

Helen I wouldn't know—and I've no desire to know.

Jack Are you sure? Are you being honest about that?

Helen This is no time for flippancy Mr——.

Jack Jack.

Helen What action are you going to take when they return?

Jack I haven't thought too much about it. I don't think I shall get my Y-fronts in too much of a twist.

Helen Meaning what?

Jack I'll not put him over my knee and spank him, that's for sure. I shall have a word.

Helen Is that all? We are talking about indecency.

Jack Are we? Are we really? What are you going to do? Stop her pocket money for two weeks and buy her a chastity belt?

Helen (*hesitating*) I shall reserve my judgment. We will wait and see where the guilt lies.

Jack Guilt? Why are we talking about guilt? Swimming without clothes on—guilt?

Helen Do I take it that you're condoning their behaviour?

Jack If I was sure what condoning meant, I'd tell you.

*Helen sweeps back to her air-bed. Maurice follows slowly. Jack and Beryl
return to their loungers*

Beryl (*to Jack*) Jack, you don't mean what you're saying. It's not right,
you know. What those two children have done isn't right.

Jack I know it's not right, I know that. But I wasn't going to agree with
her, was I. She's carrying on—being—what is it—pompous?

Beryl What are you going to say to him?

Jack To Malcolm? No idea. No idea at all. What does a father say to a
sixteen-year-old in a situation like this?

Beryl You'll have to think of something.

Jack The only thing I can think of saying is—you're a lucky boy.

Beryl Jack!

Jack Just a joke—just a joke.

Helen (*to Maurice*) This really is no joke, Maurice. How could she do
such a thing? She has been influenced by that boy, there's little doubt
about that.

Maurice He seemed quiet enough.

Helen They are the worst kind . . . the quiet ones.

Beryl (*to Jack*) I can't understand why he's done it. It's not like Malcolm.
Of course, it could be her.

Jack She seemed a quiet girl.

Beryl The worst kind are the quiet kind—my mother used to say.

Helen (*to Maurice*) One thing I have decided, as soon as Sarah returns,
we shall pack up and leave here. I'll not stop a moment longer than I
have to.

Maurice (*after a pause to collect a few words*) There was something I
wanted to talk about.

Helen Talk! I'm sure talking can wait.

Maurice I don't know about that. You see, I've been talking to Jack . . .

Helen Jack?

Maurice Jack, over there. He's offered me a position.

Helen What d'you mean—a position?

Maurice He's invited me to work for him.

Helen You work for him? How ridiculous! When did he ask you that?

Maurice A little while ago. When you were away.

Helen I assume you told him no.

Maurice I told him I would think about it—and have a word with you.

Helen There's nothing to think about, surely. You cannot work for him.

Maurice Why not?

Helen I would have thought it obvious why not. There's nothing he can
offer you worthy of your standing.

Maurice That may be so.

Helen Maurice, please be serious. This is not the time for silliness.

Maurice I don't think it's silly.

Helen Well I do.

Maurice It's certainly worth considering—at least that's what I think.

Helen Have you told him you're looking for a job?

Maurice No. Well, I have, in a way . . .

Helen In what way?

Maurice (*improvizing*) I said . . . well, I just mentioned I may be looking for something—in the near future.

Helen Was it necessary to tell our business to an absolute stranger?

Freda and Arnold enter. They are both amused. Freda carries a battered and tarnished bugle

Freda Hello, hello, hello! Look what I've found.

Jack A bugle!

Freda A bugle! Tah! Tiddy! Dah!

Jack Beryl, look at this. It's the same as the one I used on the beach.

Freda Is it the same, Dad, really?

Jack Really. Exactly, isn't it Beryl?

Freda There you are Arnold, didn't I say?

Arnold Indeed you did say.

Jack (*taking the bugle*) It could be the same one.

Freda I said it was the same kind of bugle—that's why I bought it. Isn't that right, Arnold?

Arnold shrugs and distances himself

Jack You bought it?

Freda For you. We saw it in a second-hand shop in the town. I guessed it was a bugle like that. I thought you'd like it.

Jack You bought it for me?

Freda Yes.

Jack Beryl, isn't that really something? D'you know, I believe all the dents in it are the same as mine at home. It could be my old bugle.

Freda Maybe it is.

Jack No, mine is still at home—up in the loft somewhere. (*He wipes the inside of the bugle with his fingers. Then suddenly*) Beryl, I'm going to have a go at blowing this.

Beryl Jack, not now . . .

Jack Why not? (*He moistens his lips etc. then blows an unsteady note*) What about that then?

Beryl Jack, not now . . . please!

Jack It's all right. Nothing wrong with that. I'll try to blow the old rallying call. Freda, d'you remember the old rallying call?

Freda No, I don't.

Jack Come on! Come on now! Think!

Freda I don't—really.

Jack Beryl, how did the rallying call go?

Beryl's reply is cut short by Jack's vocal rehearsal

Tah-tah, tiddy tah . . . Do you remember that, Freda?

Freda (*still amused*) No, I don't.

Beryl Of course she doesn't. (*She gives Freda a look*)

Jack Kids never forget things like that—(*he moves close to Maurice*)—do they Maurice? I used to blow a bugle on the beach . . . when these two were young. Isn't that right, Beryl? Calling them in when I couldn't find them. I bet you never did that.

Maurice No I didn't. But, Jack . . .

Jack Yes?

Maurice I'll take that job if you'll have me.

Jack It's yours. It's yours, Maurice. We'll talk later on. All right?

Maurice Right. (*He returns to his chair uneasily*)

Jack (*returning to his camp*) Now listen to this. (*He blows a far from perfect call*) That wasn't bad. Did you recognize it, Beryl?

Beryl I don't know. Now please sit down. The whole beach will be looking at us.

Jack (*grumbling*) Well . . . all right, but who's going to stop a galloping horse——

Freda ⎫
Jack ⎭ (*together*)—to look at us. (*Another family joke*)

Jack sits down and examines the bugle

  Sarah and Malcolm enter

Helen Well really, Maurice, what are those people going to do next? Is there no end to their vulgarity? (*She sees Sarah and Malcolm*) So there you are.

Sarah Yes.

Jack and Beryl see them

Helen Come here.

Sarah Why?

Helen Why? Because I said so.

No movement from Sarah

  Why are you standing there? What are you doing?

Sarah Nothing.

Helen I wish to speak to you.

Sarah I know that.

Helen Well?

Sarah We're staying together.

As if pre-arranged they sit on the sand—still holding hands

Beryl (*to Jack*) Jack, what are you going to do?

Jack These two are playing it very clever.

Helen (*to Maurice*) What does she mean?

Maurice Umm?

Helen Staying together.

Maurice Staying together—on the beach—perhaps.

Helen Your friends, over there, are saying and doing nothing.

Jack (*to Beryl*) I'm not sure what we can do.

Beryl They're holding hands.

Jack I told you—they are playing very clever. United they stand, divided they fall.

Helen Maurice, will you do something?

Maurice Well, I'll certainly try. I'll have a word with her. (*He begins to stand up*)

Helen (*stopping him*) No. Not while they're staying together. Sit down. We don't want any fuss.

There is a pause. Jack stands

Jack Malcolm, old son, I'd like to have a word with you—when you're free, that is.

Malcolm (*to Sarah*) I believe my father may understand.

Jack (*overhearing*) I wouldn't be too sure about that. I find it very hard to understand, as a matter of fact.

Helen stands up

What came over the pair of you?

Helen Thank you, but I can question my own daughter, if you don't mind. Come along Sarah. (*She grips Sarah's arm*) I wouldn't stay there if I were you.

Sarah (*firmly*) Let go of my arm!

Helen I beg your pardon! Who do you——?

Sarah (*raising her voice*) Let go of my arm!

Helen Sarah, please don't be silly.

Sarah (*with rising anger*) Let go! Let go! Don't you dare touch me, or I'll scream!

Maurice I say . . .

Sarah's short but violent outburst shakes Helen—but she maintains control. Beryl stands up. The four adults stand coupled each side of the children

Helen Sarah, you will behave yourself. Whatever next. We'll be the talk of the beach.

Sarah Why all the fuss? Why?

Helen You don't know? Of course you know. And we are not making a fuss. You were swimming without clothes.

Sarah So?

Helen "So?" What do you mean—"So?"

Sarah Is it a crime?

Beryl It's hardly the thing—not the thing to do.

Helen That is an understatement, if ever I heard one. It's indecent, that's what it is.

Jack Malcolm, you've never done this sort of thing before.

Malcolm Yes I have.

Helen There you are! I knew it . . .

Jack (*ignoring Helen*) You've swum in the nude before?

Malcolm Yes.

Beryl Malcolm, you haven't.

Helen I knew he was responsible.

Jack (*to Malcolm*) When?

Malcolm Last year—on holiday with the school.

Jack With girls?

Malcolm A few.

Helen Then it is obvious that Sarah has been led on by your son.

Sarah I was not. I've done it before as well.

Helen Sarah, please do not make it worse by telling lies.

Sarah I am not telling lies. It was when I was staying with Penelope—at Bognor Regis.

Helen Penelope? Penelope Saunders? I don't believe it. Her father is a Methodist Minister!

Sarah It's true. Her brother and his friend were there . . .

Helen (*to Maurice*) Well, really! Who *do* you know these days? You remember the Saunders?

There is a pause. The two sets of parents brooding over their fledgelings exchange almost sympathetic glances

Beryl (*to Jack*) Are you going to do something? Or are we just going to stand here?

Jack (*raising his voice*) What d'you suggest? I box his ears, stop his pocket money, spank his ass?

Helen Vulgarity will not help the situation.

Beryl moves in close to Malcolm and Sarah

Beryl Now listen to me. What's the idea? Are you going to sit there for the rest of the holiday—what's left of it?

Jack (*looking at his watch*) It's nearly five o'clock.

Malcolm We shall stay here until you stop making a fuss.

Jack I told you! It's what they call political aggression, passive insurgence. It's on the telly every night.

Beryl (*to Malcolm*) You're doing this to stop us making a fuss?

Malcolm In a way. It's our only defence.

Jack Defence? I will slap your ass!

Beryl (*calmly*) You can't sit here for ever.

Malcolm (*after a pause*) We're going to see each other when we get home. They live just ten miles from us.

Helen Ten miles is much too far.

Malcolm I don't think so.

Sarah Neither do I.

Maurice Ten miles is not far at all—if you have transport.

Helen Quiet, Maurice! Sarah, you will forget travelling ten miles to pursue—a—a friendship.

Jack Aren't we good enough for you again?

Helen Frankly, Mr . . . ah——

Jack Jack.

Helen Mr——?

Jack Mercer.

Helen Mercer. Frankly, you are not our type at all. And what's more, my daughter already has more than enough friends, and I see no point in augmenting the list at this moment in time. Also, I understand you have offered my husband a position in your garage. It's a very kind gesture, meant in the best possible way, I'm sure, but he is unable to accept. You see, he has numerous other offers to consider, some of which are more suited to his experience and qualifications.

Maurice That is not true.

Helen I beg your pardon, Maurice. What is not true?

Maurice I have nothing . . . (*fading*) . . . to consider.

Jack And he is worrying himself sick about it. The job I'm offering would suit his experience and—what was it?—qualifications. All that's not suitable would be his image. He wouldn't be Financial Director. Although we could call him Director of Finance. Would that help the image?

Helen How impertinent! Maurice what have you been telling people? I'm sure you're not interested in Mr Mercer's proposition.

Maurice Yes, I am. I would like to give it a try.

Jack Well done, Maurice.

Maurice I have nothing else to try.

Helen You have.

Maurice I have not—and you know I haven't.

Helen (*angrily*) I know no such thing! And don't you speak to me in that manner!

Sarah (*standing*) Will you both stop it!

Malcolm stands. Sarah takes his hand and leads him up the slope of the beach. They sit, still holding hands. There is a sudden silence. Embarrassment on both sides. Helen and Maurice return to their seats, Beryl to the lounger

Jack (*suddenly*) I know what! I'll blow the rallying call. (*He picks up the bugle*)

Beryl Jack, don't be silly.

Jack That should bring him running, eh? Ready? (*He blows a wavering call—ludicrously cutting across the situation*) Is he coming in? Do you see him? (*He is suffering slightly again. He rubs his chest*)

Beryl Jack, for heaven's sake—sit down.

Jack I think I will. (*He sits*)

Beryl Are you all right?

Jack I'm fine—fine.

Beryl Have you got a pain or something?

Jack Just a bit puffed—that's all. (*To Freda*) Freda, this really is a great bugle. Do you remember me blowing this thing when you were a kid? Eh?

Freda No, I'm sorry, but I don't.

A glance from Beryl

Jack But you must do . . .

Beryl Of course she does.

Freda Well—well, I'm not sure. Maybe I do have some recollection.

Helen (*to Maurice*) What an embarrassing situation.

Maurice He used to play a bugle on the beach.

Helen That doesn't surprise me.

Maurice He told me.

Helen You really must forget all thoughts of working for him.

Maurice But I've told him.

Helen Yes, I know. You are most certainly not going to work in a garage.

Maurice I shall be working in an office.

Helen (*beginning to show some emotion*) You are a chartered accountant. You seem to have forgotten that. (*She pauses*) How are we going to resolve all this? Sarah sitting there locked to the son, and you threatening to work for the father.

Maurice I see little wrong in that.

Helen You see little wrong in anything. I wish I had never set eyes on this beach.

Jack (*to Beryl*) D'you know, this is the best present I've had for many a day.

Beryl Thank you . . .

Jack It really is.

Beryl That's not saying much for the presents I give you.

Jack Well . . . you know what I mean. (*He caresses the bugle*) It's brought the old times flooding back. (*He pauses to reflect*) They were good days. D'you know—it really feels like the old bugle.

Beryl Are you feeling better now?

Jack Yes, I think so.

Beryl It's been a funny day—well, an odd day.

Jack Not our usual sort of day.

Beryl Nothing like.

Jack I've not had an ice-cream. Haven't had a swim—haven't read the newspapers—but I've got a bugle.

There is a pause. Freda remains standing and fidgets

Freda Dad?

Jack Um?

Freda There's something I think you should know.

Jack And what's that?

Freda When we go back home—the day after tomorrow—I shall not be coming with you.

Jack How d'you mean?

Freda Now don't get upset—but I'm staying here with Arnold.

Jack Arnold? What d'you mean, staying here with Arnold? (*He stands*)

Freda What I just said. I'm going to stay with him—for a little while anyway.

Jack (*to Arnold*) I take it this is your idea?

Arnold (*calmly*) Actually, no—it's not my idea.

Freda It was mine.

Arnold Freda suggested that she should move in. I have no objections. She must pay her way—do the chores . . .

Jack And share the bed I suppose.

Arnold Only if she wants to.

Jack You couldn't share a tandem with her! She's my daughter!! She's too good for you!

Beryl (*trying to restore calm*) Freda, is this just an extended holiday?

Freda I don't know. It may be that. It all depends.

Jack (*exploding*) What the hell is happening to my family? Will somebody tell me? I . . . (*He begins to suffer again*)

Beryl You're getting yourself into a state again. Come and sit down.

Jack (*distressed*) She's my daughter. I have always had plans for her. She is not going to start her life like this. (*He sits on the side of the lounger with his back to Freda*)

Beryl (*to Freda*) I'm not sure that I understand you. Are you going to marry him?

Freda Of course not.

Beryl But are you sure you know what you're doing?

Freda No. I'm not sure what I'm doing. But I must do something.

Beryl Why?

Freda (*strongly*) Because I'm stifled! Stifled! You don't understand that, do you?

Beryl (*calmly*) Yes. Yes, I do understand that. I understand that very well.

Freda drops her head and turns away. Helen crosses to the Mercer camp

Helen Mr—er—Mercer?

Jack (*looking up*) Yes?

Helen I want to make it quite clear that my husband will not be accepting the position you have offered him at your establishment—whatever it is —garage, I believe.

Beryl turns Freda around and embraces her

Jack (*wearily*) I see. A little while ago, he told me he was taking it.

Helen Yes, I'm aware of that fact, but he has changed his mind.

Beryl becomes interested in the exchange

Jack Is that right, Maurice? You've changed your mind?

Maurice (*hesitating*) Yes. Yes, I think so. I think I have.

Beryl (*to Maurice; strongly*) You know that's not right. You haven't changed your mind. She has! (*Pointing at Helen*) She's changed it for you!

Helen Well, really! Who . . .?

Beryl (*winding herself up*) Isn't that right, Maurice?

Helen Please lower your voice.

Beryl Maurice, isn't it? You want the job, don't you? Well then get off your knees and spout it out.

Maurice I'm not on my knees.

Beryl You're always on your knees to her.

Helen Please control yourself . . .

Beryl (*her control snapping*) Why won't you let him take the job? He needs work. He wants to do something. There's a job there that he can do.

Beryl strides quickly to Maurice, takes his hand and drags him C

Jack (*perplexed*) Beryl, what are you doing?

Beryl (*shouting*) I know what I'm doing!

Helen Are you drunk or . . .?

Beryl Don't be bloody stupid! It's the middle of the afternoon! I'll be getting drunk tonight! (*She positions Maurice*) Tonight I shall get drunk. Now, Maurice, I want you to answer truthfully—truthfully. Right? Do you want the job that Jack has offered you?

Maurice glances at Helen

Don't look at her. Get out from under her skirts. Your own answer. Answer yourself. Would you like the job—or not?

Maurice I would like it—yes . . . but . . .

Beryl There you are! (*To Helen*) He would like the job.

Helen Whether he would like it is not the only consideration. You should realize that. Will you please stop interfering.

Beryl (*with continuing aggression*) I am not interfering. Yes, all right, I am interfering. But he told me—Maurice told me—that he really would like to work for us—he really did! We need someone to do it—don't we Jack?

Jack's head is hanging. He raises it slowly

My husband isn't well . . .

Jack I'm all right . . .

Beryl You see we need someone!

Helen And so you may. I'm sorry, but that is your problem. I can assure you, most certainly, that someone will not be Maurice—I shall see to that. I'm convinced that he would be—shall we say—out of place in an establishment such as yours.

Beryl My God, you really are a snobby bitch! Frankly, I don't care if he takes the job or not. I don't care! But what I do care about is the fact that he's not saying it himself. Why don't you get off his back? Let him fly a little. Open the cage. It's not natural for a man to be so dominated.

Helen Dominated? How ridiculous! You really are a very stupid woman!

Beryl (*at top pitch*) I am not a stupid woman!!! (*She slaps Helen's face*)

Beryl lowers her arm slowly. She and Helen remain quite still. But the sound of the slap triggers off sharp simultaneous movements from the others. Jack gets to his feet. Maurice and Freda move one step. Malcolm and Sarah stand up and significantly break their grasp. There is a charged pause

(*Quietly*) I'm—I'm sorry.

Helen (*after a short pause; calmly*) I shall forget that ever happened. (*Turning away*) Come Maurice, enough is enough. (*She crosses to her camp—then turns to see that Maurice has not moved*) Maurice! We must pack up here and get away from this—this beach as soon as possible.

Maurice joins Helen and they begin hurriedly collecting their things together. Helen lifts the two books from the rug. She places Sarah's book in a bag and drops Malcolm's book on to the sand

Sarah! Come along!

Sarah hesitates

Sarah!

There is a pause

Sarah (*to Malcolm; tenderly*) Goodbye . . .

A brief smile from Malcolm. Sarah reluctantly joins Helen

Helen Sarah, will you please pick up the air-bed. Please don't bother to let the air out—there isn't time.

Sarah picks up the air-bed and joins Helen in the climb up the slope of the beach. Maurice, following close behind, stops to glance at Jack

Maurice Goodbye. It has . . . it has been an interesting day.
Jack (*nodding*) Yes. Yes, it has.

Maurice moves on wearily to the top of the beach, following Helen and Sarah. They exit

There is a short pause. Malcolm is the first to move. He crosses to pick up his book from the sand. Almost simultaneously, Arnold picks up the driftwood and moves closer to Jack

Arnold (*to Jack*) Well . . . I think I'll take my leave. I have things to do. It's been a pleasure knowing you . . .
Jack Oh . . .
Arnold There's not really very much for me here. (*Backing away*) Nothing at all. I may see you again. On the other hand . . . perhaps not. Goodbye.

Arnold glances at the driftwood before placing it on the sand. He exits

Only Jack is conscious of Arnold's exit. The Mercers are alone. Jack moves to Beryl and puts his arm affectionately around her shoulder

Jack It's time we went, love. There's nothing for us here.
Beryl (*quietly*) Back to the caravan?
Jack Back to the caravan. Hitch up and get on to the road.
Beryl Home?
Jack Home. At least, that's what you and I are going to do. (*He glances at Freda*) I'm feeling very tired and weary . . .
Beryl I'll start packing up here . . . (*She breaks away*)
Jack (*firmly*) No! No, you won't do that. We'll leave all this here—where it stands.
Beryl Here? If you're not feeling too well, Jack, we can do it . . . Malcolm and Freda . . . and . . .

Jack (*emphatically*) It all stays here. I can't be bothered with it. Let's get away. (*Reflectively*) It doesn't belong to us anymore. It's finished.

Beryl If we leave it here somebody will nick it.

Jack So what if they do? They can have it. Let's hope they will be as happy with it as we were. A family on the beach ... on the sand ... beside the sea ... as happy as we *were*.

Beryl We're not leaving all of it here. There's some of my personal things. I'll be taking those.

Jack There's no time! We're going!

Beryl and Freda scramble to the camp and begin collecting their personal belongings. There is the sound of a stiffening breeze. Jack picks up the driftwood. Freda suddenly becomes aware that Arnold has gone

Freda Where's Arnold?

Jack He just left.

Freda Left?

Jack Just went off.

Freda Which way?

Jack That way—I think.

Freda Why didn't he say? Why didn't you say?

Freda hurries off

Beryl Jack, don't let her go! Stop her—for heaven's sake!

Jack It's all right, Beryl. She'll be back.

Beryl looks anxiously in the direction of Freda's exit

Beryl (*numbed*) How d'you know that?

Jack Take my word for it. She'll be back.

Beryl watches for a few seconds. Malcolm begins to move to the top of the beach. Jack places the driftwood on the sand

Come on! Come on! Let's be on our way.

He puts his arm around Beryl and they begin to move up the slope of the beach

(*Looking up*) Malcolm! I see you're carrying nothing again. (*He sounds almost like the old Jack*)

Malcolm, at the top of the beach, acknowledges Jack's call with a lazy wave of his book before moving out of view

Jack and Beryl reach the top of the beach and, without looking back, move off

The sun-loungers and wind-shields stand, carcass-like, on the sand. The breeze stiffens. There is the sound of the sea. The Lights slowly fade to a Black-out

FURNITURE AND PROPERTY LIST

SCENE 1

On stage: Impression of a sandy beach
Piece of driftwood

Off stage: Hessian carrier bag **(Arnold)**
3 sun-loungers, wind-shields, a folding table, deflated inflatables, kit-bag containing bats, balls, racquets, shuttlecocks, binoculars, hipflask of whisky, foot pump **(Jack)**
2 beach bags containing towels, sun-cream, sun-glasses, cigarettes, lighter, magazine, make-up bag with make-up, mirror and comb, flask of coffee, cups, plastic tray, cans of Coke, tissues **(Beryl)**
Beach bag, camera **(Freda)**
2 tabloid newspapers, paperback copy of *The Mayor of Casterbridge* **(Malcolm)**
Tartan rug, wood and canvas chair, cushion **(Maurice)**
Duffel bag, deflated air-bed, hardback copy of *The Mayor of Casterbridge* **(Sarah)**
Holdall containing small knitted rug, *The Daily Telegraph*, book, packet of shortbread, handbag with purse and money (*Helen*)

Personal: **Maurice:** wrist-watch, pen
Jack: wrist-watch, key

SCENE 2

Off stage: Hamper. *In it:* plastic crockery, glasses, bottle of wine, food **(Beryl and Helen)**
Personal: **Arnold:** book of poetry (*for Scene 3*)

SCENE 3

Reset: Picnic items in hamper
Packet of shortbread by **Helen**
Off stage: Key **(Freda)**

SCENE 4

Off stage: Bugle **(Freda)**

LIGHTING PLOT

Property fittings required: nil
Exterior. A beach. The same scene throughout

SCENE 1 Early morning
To open: General effect of morning sunshine

Cue 1   **Jack:** "Only the sea."   (Page 17)
           Slow fade to Black-out

SCENE 2 Late morning
To open: General effect of late morning sunshine

Cue 2   **Jack** drops his paper on to his chest and stares at **Arnold**   (Page 36)
           Slow fade to Black-out

SCENE 3 Early afternoon
To open: General effect of early afternoon sunshine

Cue 3   **Maurice:** ". . . for telling me that."   (Page 48)
           Slow fade to Black-out

SCENE 4 Late afternoon
To open: General effect of late afternoon sunshine

Cue 4   **Jack** and **Beryl** exit   (Page 61)
           Pause, then slow fade to Black-out

EFFECTS PLOT

The sounds of the sea and sea-birds, etc., are not continuous throughout the play. Such effects must be used at the director's discretion to punctuate and complement the action and dialogue.

SCENE 1

Cue 1   **AS CURTAIN rises**   (Page 1)
           Sea Sounds

SCENE 2

No cues

SCENE 3

No cues

SCENE 4

Cue 2   **Beryl** and **Freda** begin collecting their belongings   (Page 61)
           Sound of stiffening breeze

Cue 3   **Jack** and **Beryl** exit   (Page 61)
           Breeze stiffens; sea sounds

MADE AND PRINTED IN GREAT BRITAIN BY
LATIMER TREND & COMPANY LTD PLYMOUTH
MADE IN ENGLAND